THEY
WERE
THERE

Confederate Camp. A painting by Conrad Wise Chapman.
The Confederate Museum.

Other Civil War Books

by PHILIP VAN DOREN STERN

The Man Who Killed Lincoln

The Drums of Morning

An End to Valor:
The Last Days of the Civil War

Editor of:

The Life and Writings of Abraham Lincoln

The Assassination of President Lincoln
and the Trial of the Conspirators
(the original Pitman report)

Secret Missions of the Civil War

The Secret Service of the Confederate States in Europe
or How the Confederate Cruisers were Equipped
by James D. Bulloch

THEY WERE THERE

The Civil War in Action

as Seen by its Combat Artists

by PHILIP VAN DOREN STERN

With 6 poems by Walt Whitman

CROWN PUBLISHERS, INC · NEW YORK, N.Y.

ACKNOWLEDGMENTS

In addition to the people and institutions mentioned in the List of Plates, the editor wishes to acknowledge his indebtedness to the following: Lloyd Goodrich of the Whitney Museum of American Art for information about Winslow Homer and Thomas Nast and general advice and counsel; R. Gerald McMurtry, of the Lincoln National Life Foundation, for Thomas Nast material; David C. Mearns, Chief of the Manuscript Division, Library of Congress, for permission to reproduce the painting by O. P. H. Balling "Grant and His Generals"; Jay Monaghan, of the University of California, Santa Barbara College, for information about the Wyles Civil War collection; Mrs. Elizabeth R. Nast for diligently searching her family records for Civil War drawings by Thomas Nast; Allan Nevins for his kindness in making a selection of the Benson J. Lossing drawings at the Henry E. Huntington Library and having them microfilmed; and Bell I. Wiley, of Emory University, Georgia, for information as to the whereabouts of certain collections of Civil War art.

The drawing on the title page of a Union soldier loading his musket is by Winslow Homer, courtesy Cooper Union Museum. The drawing below is by Edwin Forbes, courtesy Library of Congress.

Second printing, May, 1961

TABLE OF CONTENTS

LIST OF PLATES

COLOR PLATES

BLACK-AND-WHITE PLATES

INTRODUCTION

For nearly half a century after the end of the Civil War American taste was at a very low level. It was the age of the whatnot and the bustle, the era of derivative and overly ornate architecture. Hundreds of memorials to the heroes of the war were erected, most of which were so clumsily executed that people now consider them absurd. And a thriving business was carried on by studio painters who were commissioned to do large set pieces to commemorate battles they had never seen. Strongly influenced by fashionable French painters like Meissonier and Detaille, they emphasized correctness of military detail. Today their large and lifeless canvases can be found only in men's clubhouses, public buildings, and storage warehouses.

The lack of artistic merit in the sculpture and painting done by these commemorative commissionaires has led the public to believe that all Civil War art is equally bad. Fortunately, it is not. Much good contemporary work was looked down upon as being crude and "unfinished." Since no one was interested in it until quite recently, it was hidden away for nearly a century. As more and more of it emerges from obscurity, critics now admit that all Civil War art is not necessarily as bad as it was painted.

Basically there are two kinds of contemporary Civil War art. One was made by trained draughtsmen like Winslow Homer, Edwin Forbes, and the Waud brothers, who were sent into the field to make on-the-spot sketches for the pictorial press. The other was made by amateurs who had little or no formal training in art. These were soldiers, sailors, and civilians who felt that what they saw was worth recording in pictorial form. They did the best they could, and their naïve work ranges from very bad and clumsy drawings to true primitives of great interest.

The field sketches made for the pictorial press were often discarded after being engraved and printed. Since few people then understood their historical importance or artistic merit, hundreds—and perhaps thousands—of priceless original drawings were destroyed as so much waste paper.

The amateurs' work had an even slighter chance for survival. Their crude pictures, which bore little resemblance to the technically proficient professional drawings and paintings of the Victorian era, were regarded as worthless. Those who inherited them were often ashamed of such seemingly childish work, so they got rid of them. Only a few remain.

The camera also caused the work of the contemporary artists to fall into disfavor. The Civil War was not only the first major conflict to be photographed widely, it was photographed with such sharp detail and realistic rendering of texture that the camera prints made other kinds of pictorial representation unpopular. Photography was still a novelty in the nineteenth century, and people admired its slice-of-life realism. Now that it has become an everyday affair, its silver miracles no longer seem so startling. As a result, new interest is being shown in the work of the combat artists.

Their output cannot compare in sheer bulk with the camera's. Frederick Hill Meserve, who has assembled one of the world's largest collections of original Civil War photographs, estimates that (including portraits) some twenty or twenty-five thousand examples exist. Contemporary drawings and paintings are far less numerous. Only a few thousand are in public collections; hardly any are in private hands.

Some of the original sketches made for the pictorial press were sold for charity at the Sanitary Fairs which were the forerunners of our modern Red Cross money-raising efforts. But most of them were destroyed just as unwanted magazine and advertising illustrations are disposed of now. The Library of Congress has what remains of the field sketches made by A. R. and William Waud, Edwin Forbes, and a few others. The New York Public Library has a group of the drawings made for *Leslie's Weekly*, and the Cooper Union Museum owns some of the sketches Winslow Homer did for *Harper's Weekly*. Harvard University has twenty-nine of the many drawings which *The Illustrated London News* sent Frank Vizetelly to America to do. And the Valentine Museum of Richmond, Virginia, owns a large collection of pictures made by the well-known Confederate artist Conrad Wise Chapman. Among them are scenes of life among the forts and big coastal guns guarding Charleston Harbor. And the Confederate Museum in Richmond has some of Chapman's paintings. Careful search has turned up no other large collections of field sketches, except those made by Benson J. Lossing as the basis for the illustrations used in his three-volume *Pictorial Field Book of the Civil War*. Several hundred of these are preserved at the Henry Huntington Library. Since Lossing visited the scenes after the fighting was over, most of his drawings tend to be static. They are pictures of places, not of people.

The amateurs' drawings were even more difficult to locate, and when found were usually small in number. Their subject matter consists mostly of scenes of life in camp, prison, in coastal batteries, and on shipboard. Relatively few show scenes of actual combat. The same Samuel Chamberlain who did a series of entertaining color drawings of the Mexican War lived on to cover the Civil War in pictures—not, unfortunately, in color. The West Point Museum has a good-sized collection of them. The Illinois State Historical Library has a number of soldier drawings, among which is a series made by Elmer Ellsworth of the Zouave uniform he helped to make famous. Since Ellsworth traveled with Lincoln from Springfield to Washington in 1861 and was one of the first officers to be killed in the war—with a funeral in the White House—his drawings, amateurish as they are, have more than ordinary interest.

Perhaps the commonest subject seen in Civil War art is the naval battle with ships blazing away at each other. There are so many of these that they seem monotonous. Much scarcer, and far more interesting, are drawings of life on the ships that fought the battles. The Mariners Museum in Newport News, Virginia, was able to supply some made by Robert Walter Weir, Jr., when he was assistant surgeon on the United States sloop-of-war *Richmond*.

Scarcest of all are pictures involving civilians. Yet we know that many such drawings were made, for dramatic pictures of the New York Draft Riots, of numerous Sanitary Fairs, of elections, of the visit of the Russian Fleet, and of wartime scenes in Washington, New York, Richmond, and smaller places appeared in the pictorial press, so preliminary sketches must have been made for the wood engravers to follow. Apparently they were thought less worthy of preservation than the battle scenes and therefore were probably destroyed during or soon after the war.

Most of the drawings that did survive were badly kept. Many were folded and creased, scuffed, and exposed to dampness and dust. Since they were often made on any kind of paper that came to hand, they deteriorated rapidly. No effort was made to keep pencil lines from rubbing. As a result of long neglect, a great many of the Civil War drawings still extant are faded, worn, dog-eared, stained, grimy, and so brittle that they break into pieces. Some have become so gray that it is almost impossible to reproduce them.

The oil paintings fared better. They were more highly regarded than the drawings and were usually kept hanging on walls instead of being stored away in damp cellars or hot, dusty attics. The canvas on which they were painted is more durable than cheap paper, and it is easier to restore a painting than it is a pencil drawing. Relatively few paintings of Civil War interest were made during the years of conflict.

It was impossible to set up canvas and work on it in the midst of battle, so most of the wartime paintings are of quieter scenes such as life in camp or prison, where the men had plenty of time to record their impressions of what was going on. The few soldier paintings we have were usually done in watercolors, the materials for which were easier to carry than the more elaborate equipment required for oil painting.

One of the best and largest collections of soldier drawings is that made by John T. Omenhauser while he was a Confederate prisoner of war in the Federal detention camp at Point Lookout, Maryland. There are 46 of these lively watercolors in the album now owned by the Maryland Historical Society. The Society also has a group of black-and-white drawings of prison scenes made by Allen C. Redwood. And it has many original sketches for the celebrated series of etchings produced by the satirical Confederate artist, Adalbert John Volck ("V. Blada").

There are more Volck drawings in the M. and M. Karolik collection of Civil War art in the Museum of Fine Arts in Boston. This superb group of nearly 200 pictures is being cataloged for public exhibition. When it is put on view, it will be seen that it is second in importance only to the greatest of all collections of Civil War art—that of the Library of Congress.

The pictorial press used both drawings and photographs as copy. Since there was then no way of reproducing large quantities of anything with the delicate gradations of tone found in photographs, drawings, and paintings,* only an

---

* A fair rendering of tonal gradation could be obtained by using lithography, but the hand-drawn stones had to be printed in a press which was so slow that it could turn out only 300 copies a day. The rate of production for printing from copper plates such as mezzotints and etchings was even slower.

Illustrations could then be reproduced in large quantities only by using wood engravings. The pictorial press of the day organized the production of these engravings to a point of great efficiency. Drawings sent in by field artists were traced on a block of smoothly surfaced boxwood; photographs had to be redrawn in line. A large block was made up of a number of small rectangular sections held together by sunken bolts and nuts as is shown in the contemporary illustration. After the guide-drawing was completed, a wood engraver cut in all the lines which crossed from one individual section to another. The entire block was then taken apart so each section could be given to a separate engraver. In this way a number of men could work on the illustration at once. Some of them were highly specialized. One man, for instance, might do only human figures; another drew in the trees and foliage; while still another worked on architectural details. When finished, the separate pieces making up the whole

block were fastened together again. This ingenious division of labor speeded up production.

ARTIST PUTTING A PICTURE ON THE WOOD.

ENGRAVER AT WORK.

The engraved block was then locked up in a form with hand-set type from which a wax-mold electrotype was made. These electrotypes were printed as flat-bevelled plates on Taylor Cylinder Presses or were cast as curved plates to be used on the Hoe Rotary Press which could turn out 5000 sheets an hour. (Articles describing the technique of producing illustrated papers can be found in *Leslie's Weekly* for August 2, 1856 and in *Harper's New Monthly Magazine* for December, 1865).

Since the pictorial press had begun in the United States during the 1850's, the Civil War was the first American war to be reported with illustrations printed soon after the battles. It was the insatiable demand for pictorial materials for these papers that was responsible for so many field sketches being made.

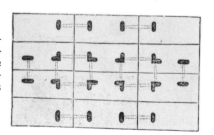

The back of a wood engraver's large block, showing how the separate sections were fastened together by nuts and bolts in sunken grooves.

Mr. E. B. Bensell of Philadelphia attended the launching of the ironclad steam frigate *New Ironsides* at Merrick & Sons' Philadelphia shipyard on May 10, 1862. He sent this sketch to *Leslie's* asking $5 in Pennsylvania or New York currency as payment if his drawing was used.

Leslie's bought the drawing; their artists and engravers came up with this much showier wood engraving which may have been more interesting to their readers but which is far less authentic than the original. Note the exaggerated display of flags and the different background.

approximation of the original could be produced by engraving it on wood so it could be printed rapidly and cheaply on the highly developed steam-powered presses of the day. These presses were remarkably productive. A normal issue of *Harper's Weekly* had a circulation of about 125,000 copies which could be turned out in two days. Special numbers ran as high as 300,000 copies.

What these high-speed presses produced, however, was often very different from the original copy. Much was lost in the hurriedly made engravings, more was lost in the press run. But no one then thought of the original drawings as art—they were simply guides for the engravers to follow. The field artists, knowing this, often did not finish their sketches. They gave written instructions about details that could be added or elaborated upon in the engraving shop. Many of these notes can still be seen on the drawings.

Since everything pictorial had to be printed from woodcuts, engravings, etchings, or hand-drawn lithographic stones, the people who lived during the Civil War seldom had a chance to see an original drawing or photograph of a battle scene. They were, however, used to looking at photographic portraits which had been popular for many years. The large, bulky, awkward cameras of the day were well suited to the portrait gallery, but they were difficult to use in the field. The photographers who did so had portable studios on wagons to carry their cumbersome equipment.

They had all been trained as portrait photographers, and they continued to make many portraits during the war. As a result, we have photographs of nearly everyone of importance in that generation as well as thousands of pictures of soldiers or people unknown. The overemphasis on the photographic portrait—from that day to this—to the great neglect of the artist's informal sketch is unfortunate. The discovery of an unpublished photograph of Lincoln is an event of national importance, yet numerous sketches of him made from life exist—and are largely ignored. It is surprising how many have been hidden away in public collections. More than a dozen are reproduced here, some of them for the first time.

The Civil War photographs had to wait for the invention of halftone printing to become widely known. A small collection was published in 1907 in a volume entitled *War Photo-*

graphs Taken on the Battlefields During the Civil War in the United States. Then, in 1911, when some 3800 of them were reproduced in the ten-volume *Photographic History of the Civil War*, they attracted such enthusiastic attention that they have dominated the pictorial representation of that war ever since.

They were so seemingly real and so interesting that hardly anyone noticed that the picture of war they presented was completely static. They never showed the shock of battle, the movement of troops on the march, a cavalry charge, a hand-to-hand struggle, or the frenzied activity of men loading and firing guns. Their still, brightly lighted, often obviously posed scenes showed what a war looked like only before a battle began or after it was over.

There was good reason for this, of course. The primitive photographic apparatus of the day was so slow that it could not stop action.* Every shot had to be a time exposure, and unless the light was reasonably strong, a picture could not be taken. That is why there are few interiors showing people, no night scenes, and no photographs at all of actual combat. They never present the war as the soldiers on the front lines saw it. Even the few photographs that were taken where fighting was going on show the face of battle with its features in calm repose.

The aesthetic limitations of photography also make the camera pictures less interesting than a good drawing. Even

---

* Civil War photographers were well aware of their camera's limitations. In order to give the semblance of arresting motion, they would sometimes pose their subjects in attitudes imitating action and have them hold the pose while the lens slowly recorded the scene. In many Civil War photographs the blurred images of moving men or other objects can be seen against the clear background of everything that remained still while the picture was being taken. In a very few instances, some genuine action was recorded by the camera. The Confederate photographer, George S. Cook, took two such pictures. In one of them a photograph of Fort Sumter, a Union shell happened to fall inside the fort to explode there while a time exposure was being made. Another is a distant view of three Union ironclads firing at Fort Moultrie. Both appear in the first volume of *The Photographic History of the Civil War*. Neither is very good; and the one of Fort Sumter has admittedly been retouched.

now, with cameras that can stop any kind of action, a photograph of a rapidly moving man or animal does not convey the impression of motion as well as a skilled artist's sketch does. This became evident in the 1870's, when Edweard Muybridge made a series of instantaneous photographs of a running horse. His pictures were of great scientific interest, for they presented an exact analysis of successive movements of the horse as they were at any given fraction of a second. But the rapidly moving horse, caught with his legs frozen into all sorts of unexpected and unfamiliar positions, did not seem to be moving. Real as he was, the horse seemed curiously unreal. Furthermore, the pictures had none of the grace and flow of line seen in artists' drawings. They made the horse look like an anatomical specimen pinned down upon a chart, lifeless, oddly contorted, and utterly static. Worst of all, in many of the pictures the animal we think of as beautiful appeared to be awkward and ugly.

An instantaneous photograph cannot do what the artist long ago intuitively learned to do to suggest motion. He combines several static moments into a single, integrated kinetic picture. And he goes even beyond this to distort certain proportions to achieve the effect he wants. These tricks of combination and distortion were known to skilled draughtsmen centuries ago, and were used by Leonardo da Vinci, Michelangelo, Dürer, Ingres, Degas, and many others.

But there is more to art than the representation of motion. The artist can arrange the various elements of his picture; he can eliminate or alter the position of anything he wishes, while the camera (used without tricks as it was during the Civil War) could record only what was actually in front of it. This power to do almost anything may sometimes impair the absolute verisimilitude of the artist's work, but it also gives him the enormous advantage of being able to emphasize that which he thinks is the most important. The drawings in this book show many examples of central figures or groups standing out prominently against purposely subordinated backgrounds. The Civil War camera could not do this. Its stopped-down lens photographed everything it saw clearly and evenly across the plate and, except in a few accidental shots where haze or smoke obscured the background, it placed almost equal emphasis on all the elements in the picture.

And, most important of all, the artist gives to his work something that even the very best photographers cannot do to the same extent even now. He imprints the force of his personality, his unique way of expressing himself, on everything he draws or paints. It is difficult—and sometimes impossible—to know who made a certain Civil War photograph, for they look very much alike. But a drawing by Winslow Homer is quite different from one by Edwin Forbes. And Conrad Wise Chapman's pictures have an unmistakably individual quality of their own.

It seems strange that the artists' pictorial presentation of the Civil War should have been neglected for so long. Except for a few drawings occasionally reproduced as illustrations in books, very little attention was paid to Civil War

art until 1944 when Lincoln Kirstein, then a private in the Army, persuaded the National Gallery of Art and the Museum of Modern Art to put on a large retrospective show of American Battle Painting from 1776 to 1918. The catalog of the exhibit reproduced fourteen Civil War paintings and two drawings. At the same time, the Library of Congress held a similar exhibition of drawings, engravings, lithographs, and photographs. In 1947 nearly 150 pictures from the Library of Congress show were reproduced in a catalog entitled *American Battle Art 1755-1918.* The Civil War section of this book included 53 pictures, of which 21 are drawings—16 of them by A. R. Waud.

In 1952, a pictorial history of the Civil War entitled *Divided We Fought* was published. This, although largely photographic, contained 98 drawings and paintings, mostly from the Library of Congress. Thirteen of them duplicated those already shown in *American Battle Art.*

In collecting pictures for the present book the editor has tried to avoid using material that appeared in those two volumes. Some duplication was necessary, however, for the two earlier books contained some Civil War drawings which are so important that they could not be ignored. But duplication has been kept to a minimum, and only a dozen pictures appear here that were in the other two volumes.

Every effort has been made to present fresh material and to show aspects of the war that have seldom been seen before. More than 90 per cent of the original drawings and paintings reproduced here have never been printed in books. Hundreds of photographs were taken of pictures all over the country so a final selection could be made. The illustrations were then chosen primarily for their artistic merit—which admittedly varies considerably—and for their historic interest. Action pictures were favored over static, although a few of the latter which show scenes not recorded by the camera have been included.

The editor has tried to present only those pictures which were made during the war—or which were worked up from wartime sketches. In some cases, however, he unknowingly may have used a drawing or painting of later date. It is impossible to give an absolute guarantee of contemporary origin, for the pictures came from all sorts of places, ranging from the carefully cataloged collections of the nation's leading museums to the storage rooms and cellars of local historical societies. In many instances little or nothing is known about the original; when it is unsigned and undated one can only guess—and hope to be right. Since this is the first attempt to assemble and appraise a large number of examples of Civil War art, a certain amount of error must be allowed for. There has been very little to go by, and the editor has often had to make a decision based only upon his knowledge of the history of the period and his ability to distinguish an artist's style of execution.

Sixty miles west of Baltimore, high up in the mountains, is Crampton's Gap, where one of the battles preliminary to the major engagement at Antietam was fought. There, in lofty loneliness stands a large, ugly stone arch. It was erected in 1896 by George Alfred Townsend, one of the best of the Civil War correspondents, as a memorial to the men who had gone into the field with him to report the progress of the war. On it are marble tablets inscribed with the names of 157 writers, photographers, and artists who had put down on paper the history of the Civil War as it was enacted from day to day.

Among the names are those of some of the artists who made the pictures in this book. But their true memorial is not that lonely, grotesque arch in the mountain wilderness. It is their works, their drawings and paintings, which show the face of war as it really was. Only they were able to catch and record the climax of battle, the strange and terrible beauty of men and horses locked in mortal combat. Some of the names of the professionals mean nothing now as do nearly all the names of the soldiers and sailors who made an amateur's pictorial record of the war. But their work lives on, a graphic account of a way of fighting that has passed into history and that now seems almost as remote as the inexorable tramp of the Roman legions and the march of Xenophon's ten thousand to the sea.

Harper's Weekly praised the Civil War artists while they were still at work. In the issue for April 30, 1864, when Grant was marshalling his forces for the great Wilderness campaign that was to begin a month later, the center spread of the paper was given over to a group of woodcuts by Thomas Nast entitled "The Press on the Field" reproduced on the opposite page. And then, near the end of the war, the same paper again paid tribute to the men who had risked their lives to make field sketches.

[They] have not been less busy, and scarcely less imperiled than the soldiers. They have made the weary marches and dangerous voyages. They have shared the soldier's fare: they have ridden and waded, and climbed and floundered, always trusting in lead-pencils and keeping their paper dry. When the battle began, they were there. They drew the enemy's fire as well as our own. The fierce shock, the heaving tumult, the smoky sway of battle from side to side, the line, the assault, the victory—they were a part of all, and their faithful fingers, depicting the scene, have made us a part also.

Thomas Nast's wood engraving in *Harper's Weekly*, "The Press on the Field." His field sketch book is at the bottom center, while an artist in action is shown in two of the five small pictures at the top (the first and fourth).

THE CIVIL WAR ARTISTS

THE MOST celebrated of all Civil War artists is Winslow Homer (1836-1910). His self-portrait, the only one he ever made, appears on page 50 (bottom right, entitled "Our Special"). This semi-humorous picture, lithographed during the war, shows him working as an artist in the field.

Homer was born in Boston of an old Massachusetts family. He grew up in Cambridge where he received only an elementary education. At nineteen he was apprenticed to John H. Bufford, the Boston lithographer. He worked in his shop for two years and so learned to draw directly on the wood for engraving. At 21,

An early self-portrait by Thomas Nast.
(New York Public Library)

he moved into his own studio where he contributed to the pictorial press, particularly *Ballou's* and *Harper's*. By 1861 he had a studio in the old New York University Building on Washington Square.

Harper's sent him to Washington to sketch the first Lincoln inauguration and then to Yorktown at the beginning of the Peninsular Campaign in 1862. It was at this time that he got most of his first-hand experience of army life. Far more interested in art than in reporting, he returned to his New York studio in the summer of 1862 and began making his first serious paintings. They were of wartime subjects worked up from his field sketchbooks. The pictures he did for *Harper's* and other periodicals during the rest of the war were largely of genre subjects, many of which are of special interest because they record the civilian life of the time. Others depict wartime activities but are of a general nature.

Aesthetically, his work is the finest of all Civil War art. It is regrettable that there is so little of it. His reputation came from the paintings and water colors of his later years, but he got his first acclaim for his pictures of soldiers in camp and battle.

Like Homer, Thomas Nast (1840-1902) gained his greatest fame for the work he did after the war, but wood engravings of his drawings published in the pictorial press during the Civil War firmly established his name with the public. Nast was born in Germany, but was brought to New York at the age of six. When he was 15, *Frank Leslie's Illustrated Newspaper* hired him for $4 a week. He got his early training there and was soon doing work for other papers as well. He toured Europe as a free-lance artist in 1860. Soon after his return in 1861, he went to Baltimore and Washington to make drawings of early wartime activities there.

He made relatively few on-the-spot sketches and became known for his large symbolic or interpretive picture like "The Press on the Field" shown here. Despite his frequent lapses into Victorian sentimentality, he could be savagely satiric and later became famous for his powerful political cartoons.

Good as they were as artists, neither Homer nor Nast contributed much toward making a detailed pictorial record of the Civil War. This was done by lesser-known men who followed the armies in the field and stayed with them year after year to sketch the day-by-day activities of the fighting man. It is to them and not to the so-called fine artists that we owe the rich pictorial record which shows almost every aspect of the great conflict.

Pre-eminent among the field artists are two brothers, Alfred R. (1828-1891) and William Waud. They made thousands of on-the-spot sketches, of which many have been preserved. Unfortunately, very little is known about them except that they were of English birth. Alfred came to America in 1858 and was employed by *Harper's Weekly* to cover the war. His work is a detailed account of the fighting in Virginia, ranging from scenes near Washington before the first battle of Bull Run to the last phases of the Appomattox Campaign. Personal details about him are so sketchy that it is not even known for what name his middle initial stands.

Still less is known about his brother William, for whom birth and death dates have not been established. His work shows that he spent most of his time sketching the war in the West and the far South although he was in Charleston before the attack on Fort Sumter and in Virginia in the summer of 1864.

The other field artist who left a large body of available drawings is Edwin Forbes (1839-1895). Unlike most of the men who sketched the Civil War, Forbes went on to make a lifetime career of the subject. He used his wartime drawings as the basis of several paintings and also of an elaborate series of etchings published under the title *Life Studies of the Great Army*. He also wrote and illustrated his reminiscences of the war in a two-volume work entitled *Thirty Years After, An Artist's Story of the Great War* (1891). Shortly before his death, he became paralyzed on the right side. He then taught himself to draw with

A. R. Waud photographed by Brady at Gettysburg. (Library of Congress

his left hand, and with the help of his wife went on to producing to the end.

The United States government had an opportunity to buy the great body of his work in 1884, when a bill was introduced in Congress to authorize its purchase. But, as so often happens when money is asked for the preservation of cultural material enough votes could not be had, and the bill was defeated.

J. Pierpont Morgan, who owned a large number of Civil War field sketches, donated them to the Library of Congress. The collection is especially rich in examples of first-rate work by the Waud brothers and Edwin Forbes.

The Wauds and Forbes were fortunate in having their work preserved. Only one other important Civil War artist, Conrad Wise Chapman (1842-1910), has had a large group of his wartime drawings and paintings kept together. Thirty-one of his small but exquisitely detailed paintings are in the Confederate Museum while the great bulk of his work is in the Valentine Museum, both in Richmond.

Chapman's father was a well-established Virginia artist whose best-known painting, "The Baptism of Pocahontas," hangs in the Rotunda of the United States Capitol. He took his son to Rome when he was six years old. The boy grew up there, and his father taught him to paint. He had become a skillful artist of the Romantic tradition when the war began. He hurried to New York and went on to Kentucky to join a Confederate regiment there. Seriously wounded at Shiloh in 1862, he was sent to Charleston where he made his celebrated series of paintings of the harbor defenses. In addition to these, he did hundreds of sketches of soldier life and many military portraits. His work is by far the best and most important of Confederate contribution to the art of the Civil War.

He returned to Rome in December 1864. While there, he learned that the Confederacy had ceased to exist as an independent government. He went to Mexico, became temporarily insane and then, after recovering, shuttled back and forth between

William Waud sketching a naval battle from the foretop of the U. S. War Steamer *Mississippi*. (*Leslie's Weekly*)

The Confederate artist, Conrad Wise Chapman, made this sketch of a picket sitting on a tree stump near the Diascund Bridge on the Chickahominy Road on March 8, 1863. He later elaborated his drawing into a painted self-portrait in which he replaced the picket's face with his own.
(Valentine Museum)

Mexico and Rome until the last years of his life, which he spent in Richmond.

Another noted Confederate artist is John Adalbert Volck (1828-1912). He was born in Germany and fled from that country after the Revolution of 1848. He spent some time in St. Louis and in the California gold rush; then he settled in Baltimore where he became a dentist.

Unlike most German refugees from the Revolution of 1848, Volck was an ardent Confederate sympathizer. He was imprisoned in Fort McHenry in 1861 by orders of General Benjamin F. Butler. In retaliation, he often caricatured Butler as well as Lincoln, who was the special target of his satire. His drawings, executed in fine, delicate lines for a series of wartime etchings, are widely scattered and very rare.

Although he did not serve the Confederacy officially, the British artist Frank Vizetelly (1830-1883?), was strongly pro-Southern. He was a younger brother of Henry Vizetelly, the wood engraver who founded several British illustrated newspapers and later became a successful book publisher. Frank, after covering Garibaldi's campaigns in Italy for *The Illustrated Lon-*

ALEXANDER MEINUNG
is one of the few soldier artists of whom a photographic portrait exists. Some of his work appears on pages 73-75.

FRANK VIZETELLY,
the artist-correspondent for *The Illustrated London News.* (Library of Congress)

don News, sailed from Liverpool to Boston on May 4, 1861, to sketch the war in America for the same paper. He was received enthusiastically in the South, where he traveled widely. At Chickamauga, General Longstreet made him an honorary captain in the Confederate Army. Some of Vizetelly's drawings, which were sent to London through the blockade, were lost at sea; others, captured by Union warships, were promptly pirated in the Northern press.

After the war, Vizetelly went to Egypt. He disappeared in 1883, and is believed to have been sold into slavery or killed in the massacre of Hicks Pasha's army near Kashgil in the Sudan.

Hundreds of artists had wood engravings made from their work published in the pictorial press during the Civil War. A check of their names shows that Arthur Lumley, Henry Lovie, Alexander Simplot, Henry Mosler, Theodore R. Davis, John R. Hamilton, Angelo Wiser, Frank H. Schell, A. M. Cullum, A. W. Warren, and others contributed many field sketches that were reproduced as wood engravings. Early in the war the name of the artist who made the original drawing was seldom acknowledged. Very often the artists themselves did not bother to sign their sketches. Everyone connected with the production of the illustrated papers then looked upon the drawings from the field only as informative data for the wood engravers to follow. And the engravers doubtless thought that their finished products were vastly superior to the artists' hastily drawn impressions of action in the field. The men who risked their lives at the various fronts were largely forgotten. Comprehensive reference books on American art do not even list the names of most of them.

Our knowledge of their personal careers is so slight that although we know, for instance, that the highly productive Arthur Lumley was a Dublin-born Irishman who came to America before the war, even the date of his arrival is in dispute. He was born in 1837 and died in Mount Vernon, New York, in 1912. We know that Henry Mosler was born in Richmond, Indiana, and that he worked in Cincinnati as a wood engraver, but that is about all. Henry Lovie worked in the same city and was part of the firm of Lovie and Bauerle, wood engravers, for Cincinnati was an important center of this art in the years before the war.

As for the rest, their names and their pictures are usually all that remain. And in many cases the original drawings they made for the pictorial press have disappeared so that poorly printed engravings are the only records of their lost careers.

Sometimes, purely by chance, more is known about a relatively obscure artist than one would expect. This is particularly true of George W. Reed, an amateur who made hundreds of Civil War drawings. By good luck much of his work was preserved and presented to the Library of Congress where it can be seen in two large albums.

Reed enlisted in the Ninth Massachusetts Battery in 1862 and first served as a bugler. Later he was an assistant engineer at the headquarters of the 5th Army Corps. His sketches were apparently made only for his own pleasure. Later he worked them into line illustrations for a history of the battery and for *Hard Tack and Coffee*, an endlessly fascinating book on every aspect of soldier life in the Union Army.

Except for painters like Eastman Johnson, David Blythe, William Morris Hunt, and George Caleb Bingham, who made so few pictures of wartime subjects that there is little to be said about them, the short and simple story of the Civil War artists is told. Only years of intensive research on a nation-wide basis for a multi-volumed iconography of the Civil War can bring to light further data on the careers of the unjustly forgotten artists who are now completely unknown or at best shadowy figures lost in the byways or back alleys of history. Meanwhile, this book is an introduction to their work.

CIVIL WAR ART IN COLOR

EARLY ALL contemporary Civil War pictures were black and white; paintings in oil or water color actually made during the war were very few. There were, however, many lithographs which were printed in large quantities in black ink and then colored by hand. CURRIER AND IVES specialized in such work. Their pictures were almost completely imaginary, drawn by artists working in downtown Manhattan. In their spirited but highly inaccurate battle scenes the troops charge in neat, unbroken rows. Occasionally a touch of truth was added. It was known, for instance, that observation balloons, both Union and Confederate (the Confederate one was made out of silk dresses donated by women) were used at the battle of Fair Oaks, so the Currier and Ives artist naturally put a balloon in the picture. Since the lithographers wanted to sell as many prints as they could, they favored scenes involving lots of people, for soldiers—and their relatives and friends—were their best potential customers. Even better for sales possibilities than battles—which were soon over—were camps or hospitals where large numbers of men had to stay in one place for a long time and therefore might be expected to buy prints to send home.

Somewhat like the lithographers' manufactured pictures were paintings of prominent military men put together in an artificial group even though most of them may never have seen each other. This fine example of such work was painted in 1865 by O.P.H. BALLING who traveled to City Point to sketch Grant and to the Shenandoah Valley to sketch Sheridan. After Ben Butler failed to take Fort Fisher, the artist substituted for him General A. H. Terry, who later captured the key fort. Some of the other generals in the picture are: Custer, Warren, Meade, Sherman, Burnside, Hooker, Hancock, and Howard.

THE BATTLE OF FAIR OAKS, VA MAY 31ST 1862.

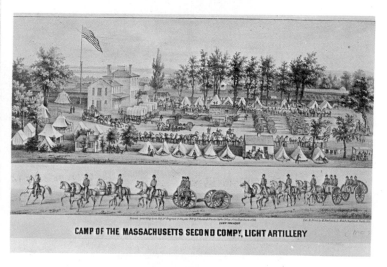

CAMP OF THE MASSACHUSETTS SECOND COMPY, LIGHT ARTILLERY

In the spring of 1862, *Harper's Weekly* sent WINSLOW HOMER to Virginia to cover McClellan's Peninsular Campaign. The young artist probably saw this memorable scene somewhere in the bitterly fought-over area between the York and the James Rivers. It made such an impression on him that he used it as the subject for one of his first paintings of the war, putting it on canvas when he returned to New York that summer. *Harper's* reproduced a wood engraving of it on November 15, 1862, under the title "The Army of the Potomac—a Sharp-Shooter on Picket Duty." It appears there almost without change, except that a canteen hanging from a branch has been added and a letter "A" appears on the top of the kepi. The Union sharp-shooter is using an extra heavy rifle equipped with a long telescopic sight.

Edwin Forbes' paintings of Gettysburg which he worked up from wartime sketches. 1. The Union defense of Cemetery Hill. 2. Artillery on Little Round Top. 3. The retreat of Lee's army in the rain.

VIZETELLY, who favored the South, visited Jeb Stuart's headquarters. His notes state that Stuart is the cloaked figure with his back to the viewer as he watches Union prisoners (not shown) being brought into camp. The man on the campstool with the plumed hat is Fitzhugh Lee. The open tent at the left is Stuart's, the one at the far right is Vizetelly's. The sketch was probably made near Martinsburg after Antietam in the autumn of 1862.

FRANK VIZETELLY, the British artist commissioned by *The Illustrated London News* to cover the war, was inside Fort Fisher when it was captured by a Union amphibious assault on January 13, 14, and 15, 1865. Its fall made Wilmington, N. C., the last major Confederate port, useless for blockade running.

Vizetelly describes the scene depicted here: "The guns at the right face the ocean and are being worked against the [Union] fleet. Shortly after the attack was made, 14 or 15 guns were... rendered useless by a concentrated enfilading fire from 15 eleven-inch cannon [pivot guns on small Federal gunboats sent in close to shore]. Your correspondent had one or two very narrow 'shaves,' and he considers himself lucky in not being taken with the garrison."

The water color shows the interior of the north-east salient of the fort as it appeared when the Federal fleet was sending in troops for a land assault. The big cannon in the right foreground is a ten-inch Columbiad. Just above it part of the Federal fleet can be seen. Behind its breech a smaller gun, probably a 6⅜-inch, has been dismounted by fire from the ships. At the extreme left a pile of cannon balls has just been hit. Behind it, men are bringing cartridge bags out of a bombproof magazine. In the left foreground a Confederate officer and two men have just been killed by shell fragments. Large round shot from the guns on the Federal gunboats are bouncing along the sand. And big shells detonated by pre-set time-fuses are exploding overhead.

Confederate prisoners being attacked on Pennsylvania Avenue, Washington. VIZETELLY said: "There was a general impression among the disorganized Federalist soldiery, after the [first] battle of Bull Run, that their wounded had been inhumanly treated by the Confederates. The most atrocious falsehoods had been circulated in reference to this in many journals . . . to increase the hatred between the North and the South."

CONRAD WISE CHAPMAN'S paintings of the Charleston Harbor area. 1. Sunset at Fort Sumter after the Federal bombardment of 1863. 2. One of the Confederate torpedo boats which proved to be more dangerous to the men who operated them than to the Federal fleet.

REBELS SWALLOWING THE OATH.

CONFEDERATE VARIETYS.

though very little is known about JOHN T. OMENHAUSSER except that he was a Confederate prisoner of war, the 46 primitive water colors he made while in the Federal detention camp at Point Lookout, Maryland, are some of the best and liveliest records we have of life in a Northern prison. Point Lookout was the only Federal detention camp that had no stone or wooden buildings. Only tents provided shelter for a prison population that was sometimes as high as 20,000. The camp was established on August 1, 1863, probably to hold some of the many captives taken a few weeks before at Gettysburg. It was located on a long, low-lying peninsula where the Potomac flows into Chesapeake Bay. The drinking water, taken from shallow wells, was so brackish that fresh water had to be shipped in by boat. In winter the area was cold and damp, but in summer, as Omenhausser's drawings indicate, life must have been fairly pleasant there. The men were allowed to bathe on the sandy beach and to supplement their rations by catching fish and crabs. Many of the Confederates who came from inland places had never seen a crab and were dubious as to whether such uninviting looking creatures were fit to eat.

Efforts were made to persuade the prisoners to take an oath of allegiance and be paroled. In 1864, Point Lookout became a feeder for City Point, where flag-of-truce boats carried exchanged prisoners to Richmond.

The ingenuity of the American mechanic is shown in the picture of an operating steam engine constructed in camp of metal from melted-down musket balls, a discarded camp kettle, stove pipe, a vegetable box, bricks, and odds and ends of lumber.

The prisoners were apparently given a pretty free hand. They organized their own entertainments and put on such diversions as a black-face minstrel show.

Except for the signature L. FINGER and the date July '63 painted on the rock at
the left, nothing is known about this charming primitive painting of a Union
surveying and mapping party at work in the field. The fort on the hill may offer
some clue to the location of the site which is said to be in a coastal area.

This gory primitive painting by JOHN W. GRATTAN is believed to represent
Fort Fisher after its capture by Federal forces in January 1865. Grattan was an
Acting Ensign on Admiral David Dixon Porter's staff and doubtless went ashore
after the battle to inspect what was left of the port.

THEY WERE THERE

Confederate fencers. By CONRAD WISE CHAPMAN. Courtesy The Valentine Museum.

This spirited drawing by WINSLOW HOMER shows men and officers in a skirmish at Lee's Mills on April 16, 1862, during the siege of Yorktown. The men, standing in close ranks, are loading and firing muzzle-loading guns and are brandishing their ramrods as they rapidly clean out the barrels and then push home a bullet for the next shot.

MEN

N WAR

Reviewing Rhode Island and Maine troops.
A painting by JAMES WALKER.

THE ARMING OF THE NATION

To the drum-taps prompt,
The young men falling in and arming,
The mechanics arming, (the trowel, the jack-plane, the blacksmith's
    hammer, tost aside with precipitation,)
The lawyer leaving his office and arming,
    the judge leaving the court,
The driver deserting his wagon in the street, jumping down,
    throwing the reins abruptly down on the horses' backs,
The salesman leaving the store, the boss, book-keeper,
    porter, all leaving;
Squads gather everywhere by common consent and arm,
The new recruits, even boys, the old men show them
    how to wear their accoutrements, they buckle the straps carefully,
Outdoors arming, indoors arming, the flash of the musket-barrels,
The white tents cluster in camps, the arm'd sentries around,
    the sunrise cannon and again at sunset,
Arm'd regiments arrive every day, pass through the city,
    and embark from the wharves. . . .
The blood of the city up—arm'd! arm'd! the cry everywhere,
The flags flung out from the steeples of churches
    and from all the public buildings and stores,
The tearful parting, the mother kisses her son,
    the son kisses his mother,
(Loth is the mother to part, yet not a word
    does she speak to detain him,)
The tumultuous escort, the ranks of policemen preceding,
    clearing the way,
The unpent enthusiasm, the wild cheers of the crowd for their favorites,
The artillery, the silent cannons bright as gold,
    drawn along, rumble lightly over the stones,
(Silent cannons, soon to cease your silence,
Soon unlimber'd to begin the red business . . .)
War! an arm'd race is advancing!
    the welcome for battle, no turning away;
War! be it weeks, months, or years,
    an arm'd race is advancing to welcome it.

—WALT WHITMAN

THE HIGH COMMAND

At the beginning of the war, the United States Army had less than 17,000 men. Virginia-born Lieutenant-General Winfield Scott, seventy-five years old and so corpulent that he could not mount a horse without help, was in command of this skeleton force. It was, however, soon augmented by tens of thousands of volunteers. Despite his age and infirmities, Scott, who had served in the War of 1812 and the Mexican War, was an able general. One of his first moves was to offer Robert E. Lee the post of supreme field command. Lee turned down the offer to remain loyal to his native Virginia. With Scott are Colonels Henry Van Rensselaer, George W. Cullom, and Schuyler Hamilton. Drawing by A. R. WAUD.

When Lincoln went to Washington for his first inauguration it was rumored that he was to be assassinated in Baltimore. He traveled in secrecy and never got out of the train while in that city. The drawing above, made by THOMAS NAST, was therefore based on incorrect information. The one below (unsigned) is even more erroneous, for Lincoln certainly did not walk through the streets of Baltimore.

Lincoln reviews troops at the White House. The lower picture by A. R. WAUD
shows a temporary stand erected on Pennsylvania Avenue. Lincoln is at the right
and General Winfield Scott (seated) at the left of the flagpole. The occasion is
July 4, 1861, when 20,000 troops from New York marched by. The upper picture
(unsigned) shows the rear of the White House. The occasion is not known.

Gen Hooker   Pres Lincoln

Pres Lincoln reviewing the Army of the Potomac on monday

In April 1863, shortly before the battle of Chancellorsville
Lincoln went to Acquia Creek to visit General Hooker. A
review of the troops was held. The drawing above is un
signed but is probably by EDWIN FORBES. The one at the lef
is a detail from a now mutilated drawing by A. R. WAUD
Lincoln was often caricatured by artists. The painting at th
top of the opposite page by DAVID G. BLYTHE is called "Lin
coln Crushing the Dragon of the Rebellion." It portray
Lincoln as a hero. But the Confederate artist, ADALBER
JOHN VOLCK, who signed his pictures V. Blada (Adalb V
spelled backward) saw Lincoln as hesitant or cowardly. Th
symbolic drawing at the left has a pike from the John Brow
raid, a log for the rail-splitter, and a caricatured portrait c
General Winfield Scott. The drawing at the right perpetuate
the myth that Lincoln passed through Baltimore on his wa
to his first inauguration disguised in a Scotch cap. Both ar
the original sketches for a series of etchings which Volc
made for publication and sale.

The Knight of the Rueful Countenance

This sketch of Lincoln, his son Tad, and Grant, presumably made at City Point in March or April 1865 by WINSLOW HOMER, contains a curious error. It shows Lincoln without a beard, although he had had one ever since October 1860, when eleven-year-old Grace Bedell suggested that he would look better with whiskers because his face was so thin.

This drawing made at City Point on March 27, 1865, by ALBERT HUNT, shows the pensive Lincoln in a characteristic pose (scratching his right ear). On his lap is a copy of the Richmond *Dispatch*, probably smuggled out of that be-leaguered city by Grant's efficient spies.

On November 26, 1864, Seth Kinman, a California hunter,
gave the President a chair made of elkhorns. Drawing by
A. R. WAUD.

Lincoln reviews the Philadelphia Fire Zouaves. Unsigned.

General Sherman reviews his army in Savannah, 1864. By WILLIAM WAUD.

During the Grand Review in Washington at the end of the war, Custer's horse bolted when women threw flowers. Drawing by CHARLES W. REED.

This is an interesting example of the way an artist worked up a field sketch. The one below was probably made on the spot and elaborated later into the more finished drawing above. It shows Grant writing a telegram on May 4, 1864, at the beginning of the Wilderness Campaign to inform Halleck that the Union Army had crossed the Rapidan. Unsigned but probably by A. R. WAUD.

Sheridan receiving reports after the battle of Winchester, September 19, 1864. Unsigned but probably by A. R. WAUD. Below is General G. K. Warren bravely rallying his Maryland troops in the Wilderness Campaign. At Five Forks, on April 1, 1865, Sheridan removed Warren from command for slowness in bringing up the Fifth Corps. Drawing by A. R. WAUD.

People who could be blamed for the Union disaster at the first battle of Bull Run were eagerly sought for. One minor figure was Colonel James E. Kerrigan of the 25th New York Volunteers. Nine charges, including drunkenness and being friendly with the enemy, were brought against him at his court martial in Washington. He is the young man seated in front of the fireplace. By ARTHUR LUMLEY.

Confederate General John B. Hood was badly wounded in the arm at Gettysburg. A few months later at Chickamauga he was hit again, this time so badly that his right leg had to be amputated. FRANK VIZETELLY captures the very moment when the ill-starred general was struck the second time.

Here the Confederate artist ADALBERT JOHN VOLCK pillories General Benjamin Butler "safe and dry" during his expedition to capture Fort Hatteras in August 1861. Butler took the fort but ran his transports aground. (Above) Volck satirizes Butler's famous Order No. 28 issued on May 15, 1862, when he was the military governor of New Orleans. It read: "As the officers and soldiers of the United States have been subjected to repeated insults from the women (calling themselves ladies) of New Orleans, in return for the most scrupulous non-interference and courtesy on our part, it is ordered, that hereafter, when any female shall, by word, gesture, or movement, insult or show contempt for any officer or soldier of the United States, she shall be regarded and held liable to be treated as a woman of the town plying her avocation."

The order created world-wide indignation, particularly in England where Prime Minister Palmerston denounced it in the House of Commons. The general was called "Beast" Butler in the South, but his order tamed the ladies of New Orleans. Oddly enough, the city's prostitutes were so incensed that they struck back at Butler in various ingenious ways.

the Death of Reynolds Gettysburg

General John F. Reynolds was killed by a Confederate sharpshooter at the opening of the battle of Gettysburg. This drawing of his death moment was probably made by A. R. WAUD who did other sketches of the same subject.

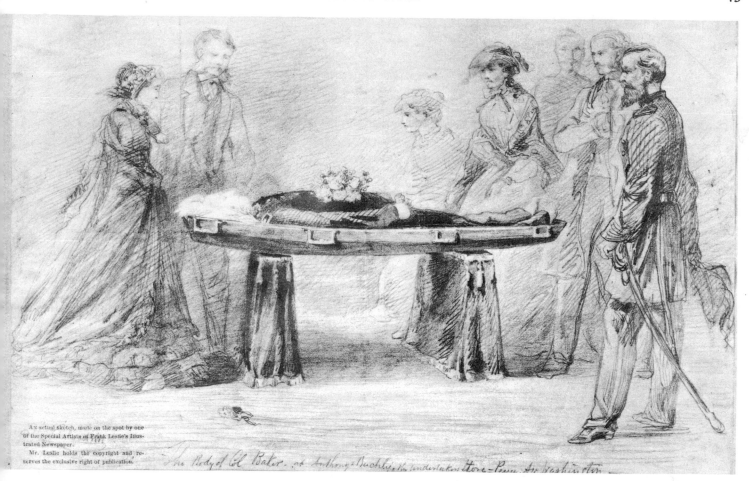

An actual sketch, made on the spot by one of the Special Artists of Frank Leslie's Illustrated Newspaper.

Mr. Leslie holds the copyright and reserves the exclusive right of publication.

The Body of Col Baker - at Anthony Buchly's undertaking store - Penn Av Washington

When Colonel (formerly Senator) Edward D. Baker, a good friend of Lincoln and a politically important public figure, was killed in the unsuccessful battle of Ball's Bluff in October 1861 his body was brought to a Washington undertaking establishment (on Pennsylvania Avenue) to lie in state. Drawing by ARTHUR LUMLEY.

On May 21, 1861, the funeral of Colonel A. S. Vosburgh, one of the first army officers to die in the war, was held in Washington. Drawing by A. R. WAUD.

After signing the surrender papers on April 9, 1865, Lee and his aide, Colonel Charles Marshall, rode away from the McLean house at Appomattox. This unsigned sketch was almost surely made by A. R. WAUD, the only professional artist who followed the Union Army in the Appomattox Campaign.

THE COMMON SOLDIER

This and the four drawings on the following two pages are part of a series made after the war by EDWIN FORBES from his field sketches for a portfolio of etchings. In them the life of the common soldier (the infantryman, the cavalryman, and the artilleryman) is shown in authentic detail. Perhaps more than any other artist, Forbes made the Civil War his career. He traveled with the armies and knew the everyday activities of the men intimately. In Plate 54, the third man on the chow line is supposed to be Walt Whitman.

A Christmas Dinner. By Edwin Forbes.

Trading with the enemy. By Edwin Forbes.

The cigar-box violin. By EDWIN FORBES.

Fall in for soup. By EDWIN FORBES.

After WINSLOW HOMER returned from the Peninsular Campaign he made a series of six black-and-white lithographs which Louis Prang and Company of Boston published in 1863. These lithographs have become exceedingly rare; only one portfolio with the original pictorial cover is known. The

six prints depict the human—and often the humorous—side
of the war. Plate 55, entitled "Foraging," shows how the
Union troops obtained food for the army. Plate 56 is entitled
"Coffee Call." In the background, soldiers attracted by the
rich aroma of hot coffee are coming in on the run.

These 24 lithographs by WINSLOW HOMER entitled "Life
in Camp" were also issued by Prang in 1864. The origina
prints, about the size of small playing cards, were done in
color and sold as packaged sets of 12 cards each. The young
man with a Vandyke beard and a broadbrimmed hat who i

BUILDING CASTLES.

HARD TACK.

UPSET HIS COFFEE.

WATER CALL.

A SHELL IS COMING.

RIDING ON A RAIL.

SURGEUNS CALL.

AN UNWELCOME VISIT.

LATE FOR ROLL CALL.

STUCK IN THE MUD.

THE GUARD HOUSE.

TOSSING IN A BLANKET.

ted on a cannon while he sketches (titled "Our Special")
Homer's only known self-portrait. He liked the scene
wn in "The Guard House" so much that he worked it up
a painting.

Here two skillful Civil War artists try their hand at portray-
ing the same kind of subject. Plate 59 is a study of a drummer boy made at Culpepper Court House on September 29,
1863, by EDWIN FORBES.

And this is a drummer boy drawn by WINSLOW HOMER. It is believed to have been made in 1864. Homer's boy seems younger and more cherubic than Forbes' more sophisticated-looking youngster.

Here again two noted Civil War figures sketch the same subject. The amateurish drawing below was made by ELMER E. ELLSWORTH who was in command of a crack Zouave company that gave exhibition drills. He was killed on May 24, 1861. This is his sketch of an early Zouave uniform.

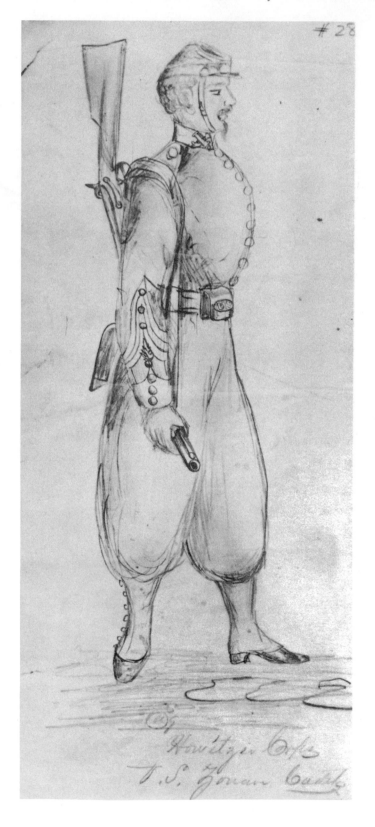

WINSLOW HOMER with assured competence draws a high professional looking Zouave who wears the uniform as appeared later in the war.

Quarter Guard

On March 10, 1863, the Confederate artist, CONRAD WISE CHAPMAN, sketched this half-frozen sentry near Diascund Bridge on the Chickahominy Road. A quarter guard, literally a guard of the quarters, was placed about 80 yards in front of the center of the camp as soon as the corps arrived.

After a heavy artillery bombardment from the heights across the river, Union troops entered the ruined streets of Fredericksburg on December 11, 1862. They had paid a heavy price to get there, and they had no hesitation in helping themselves to anything that was still intact. Some of them were charged with wanton destruction such as "bayonetting mirrors, smashing piano keys with musket butts, and pitching crockery out of windows." This on-the-spot drawing, made on December 12 by ARTHUR LUMLEY, indicates that there may have been some basis for the charge.

This pair of drawings, unsigned but perhaps by ARTHUR
LUMLEY, shows foragers roasting corn and stealing chickens.
Cavalrymen were especially adept at living off the land, for
they could roam far afield on their horses and "skim the
cream off the country."

The strange-looking box on legs is not a camera; it is a portable peep show taken from camp to camp by an itinerant showman who charged the soldiers so much a head for looking at the mysteries hidden inside the box. This box has four magnifying eyepieces, only two of which are being used at the moment. A parasol covers the instrument so the viewers can see better in its shade. Sketched at Culpepper Court House on February 11, 1864, by EDWIN FORBES.

Drunken soldiers tied up for fighting and other unruly conduct.

During the Civil War the most common offenses committed by the soldiers were: "drunkenness, absence from camp without leave, insubordination, disrespect to officers, turbulence after taps, sitting while on guard, gambling, and leaving the beat without relief." There were many ingenious ways of punishing the men for these offenses. This one was especially useful for drunkards when they could not stand on their feet. The bayonets were tied in place as gags. Unsigned.

The railroad bridge at Fredericksburg was burned before the Union attack in December 1862. A. R. WAUD, who drew this picture of it, also wrote a description: "This is a favorite spot for soldiers of either army to meet within speaking distance and exchange remarks, frequently of an uncomplimentary character. Proposals of all sorts of exchanges (impossible of accomplishment) are made, such as offers to barter coffee or tea for whiskey or tobacco. . . . The seceshers show a laudable anxiety to get New York papers for Richmond publications." One of the men is waving a copy of *Harper's Weekly*.

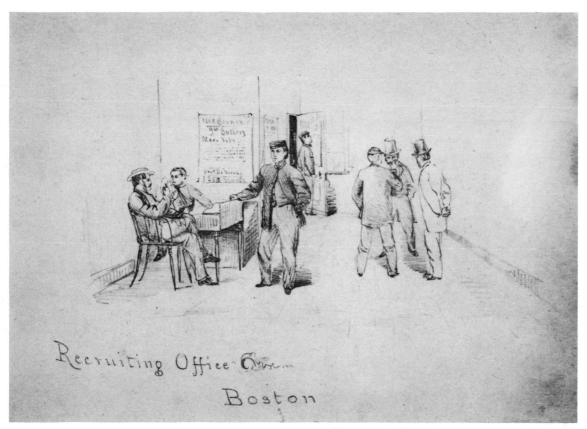

When CHARLES W. REED enlisted in the Ninth Massachusetts Battery in the summer of 1862 he drew this picture of
the interior of a Boston recruiting office complete with
posters explaining the advantages of an artillery unit.

Even before the Civil War a drinking song popular with
soldiers throughout the world was one that had the famous
toast: "And here's to the next man to die." Drawing by
A. R. WAUD.

"Detail from "Reported for duty"

"Our guard duty at Hampton, was very severe. Some of us being on Post all the time." Extract from a letter of a Family Volunteer

These four primitive drawings of soldier life in the Union Army were made by SAMUEL E. CHAMBERLAIN, whose naïve color pictures of the Mexican War were featured in three issues of *Life* (July 23, 30, and August 6, 1956) and were later published in book form. Chamberlain also took

Teaching a Baltimore Secesh manners

WARWICK COURT HOUSE. ENEMY PICKETS IN Sight. "Can you sell 10 Beeves for the troops that will camp here tonight?"

t in the Civil War, rising to the rank of Brevet Brigadier
eral. Unfortunately, his drawings of the greater conflict
e not made in color. But the same satirical touch can be
n, and despite his elevation to higher rank, his point of
w is still that of the rather cynical common soldier.

ON THE MARCH

Much of the soldier's time was spent going to or coming from places. Here (above) the men have been ordered out so suddenly that their washing did not have time to dry. One of them has hung his wet clothing on his rifle so it will dry out on the way. By EDWIN FORBES.

Again soldiers are on the move. After Chancellorsville May 1863, the enlistment period of thousands of two-ye men in the Union Army ran out. They had had enou; fighting; here (below) they crowd the trains to get hon By EDWIN FORBES.

After his disastrous defeat at Fredericksburg in December 1862, Burnside tried to redeem himself by chasing the elusive Confederates. The weather was against him. It rained torrents, and the Virginia roads became a hopeless morass. "The Mud March," January 21, 1863. By A. R. Waud.

Meade, who won the battle of Gettysburg in July 1863, also had difficulties with transportation. Here his wagons are in trouble while crossing Kettle Run on the morning of the battle of Bristoe Station, October 14, 1863. Drawing by Edwin Forbes.

The drawings of WINSLOW HOMER, which are among the finest of the Civil War, seldom illustrate a definite incident or bear a specific date. Most of them are an artist's record of war without specific allusion to time or place. From a historical point of view this is regrettable, but it makes his work seem universal and raises it above journalism. This drawing (right) is of any Union infantry column on the march, any time, anywhere.

On August 28, 1862, while falling back to Manassas for the second great battle there, Union troops under the command of General John Pope, after leaving Warrenton Junction, had to march through drenching rain. This drawing (left) by EDWIN FORBES shows how the men reacted to the heavy downpour.

Since it takes time to cut down trees, soldiers on the march
found it quicker and easier to strip farmers' fences of their
well-seasoned rails for firewood. By A. R. WAUD.

Night scene on the North Edisto River. Soldiers
crossing an improvised plank bridge. Unsigned.

When an army went into winter quarters where protection against cold weather was needed, great care was taken with the building of the camp. Shelters were made of logs chinked with mud and roofed over with planks or tent canvas. Chimneys had a pork barrel or two placed on top to add height and increase the draft. Sometimes these wooden barrels would catch fire, especially on very cold nights when wood was piled high on the hearths to provide more heat.

A cry would then run through the camp, and men would come running with long poles to knock the flaming barrel off the chimney.

This is the Army of the Cumberland going into winter quarters in the autumn of 1863. Conical Sibley tents, patterned after Indian wigwams, can be seen in the center background. By J. T. E. HILLEN.

Breaking up camp meant going on the move again, almost surely into action. Everything had to be taken down, packed up, and stowed away in wagons or knapsacks. After a long stay in one place, however, the men were usually bored enough to welcome the new activity. When the bugler sounded "The General," acres of canvas disappeared in a few minutes. The corps commander, his staff, and the color bearers then took their place where the head of the column was to be. "Attention" brought up the officers and men, and "Forward," followed by the shouted command "Right shoulder shift!" caused the whole column to start marching. Unsigned.

When the long day ended, the troops went into bivouac, which usually meant a camp for the night without shelter. The first to arrive, of course, got the best camping places. Latecomers had to take what was left. All over the field, hundreds and sometimes thousands of campfires gleamed, each one sending up a thin column of smoke. At 8:30 the bugler sounded "Attention," followed in five minutes by "Tattoo" when the final roll call for the day was taken. At nine o'clock came "Taps," followed by a few isolated drum beats which gave the call its name. Lights went out then, and only the sentries were left to patrol their lonely posts. Drawing by EDWIN FORBES.

"Bummers," as defined by General Sherman who made the word famous, are men who "serve as feelers who keep in advance and on the flanks of the main columns, spy out the land, and discover where the best supplies are to be found. They are indispensable in feeding troops when compelled, like my army, to live off the country." By NATHAN B. WEBB.

Here, and on the following two pages (Plates 88 to 91) are four primitive field sketches made by ALEXANDER MEINUNG, a musician with the 26th North Carolina Regiment Band. The one shown above is entitled by the artist: "Pioneer asleep. Worn out! In Chickahomene [*sic*] swamp—June 1864."

Pioneers had good reason to be worn out. They were expert with the ax, pick, and shovel. Their duty was to build roads, bridges, and do other hard manual labor that called for dexterity and skill with tools. As seen here, they also carried guns and often had to work under fire.

These three drawings by ALEXANDER MEINUNG show the army on the move and in camp. The first (upper one on opposite page) was made near Front Royal, Virginia, on July 23, 1863, during the Confederate retreat from Gettysburg. The men are putting a pontoon bridge across the Shenandoah River. (Lower picture) Drinking water from a brook out of a campaign hat. Made near Greenville, North Carolina, on April 18, 1863. And the one above shows a night in camp at Goldsboro, North Carolina (no date). The men silhouetted against a brightly burning campfire make a striking nocturne of a kind seldom seen in Civil War art.

And I saw askant the armies,
I saw as in noiseless dreams hundreds of battle-flags,
Borne through the smoke of the battles
   and pierc'd with missiles I saw them,
And carried hither and yon through
   the smoke, and torn and bloody.
And at last but a few shreds left on the staffs,
   (and all in silence,)
And the staffs all splinter'd and broken.

★ ★ ★

   As I wake from sleep this vision presses upon me;
The engagement opens there and then in fantasy unreal,
The skirmishers begin, they crawl cautiously ahead,
   I hear the irregular snap! snap!
I hear the sounds of the different missiles,
   the short t-h-t! t-h-t! of the rifle-balls,
I see the shells exploding leaving small white clouds,
   I hear the great shells shrieking as they pass,
The grape like the hum and whirr of wind through the trees,
   (tumultuous now the contest rages,)
All the scenes at the batteries rise in detail before me again,
The crashing and smoking, the pride of the men in their pieces,
The chief-gunner ranges and sights his piece
   and selects a fuse of the right time,
After firing I see him lean aside
   and look eagerly off to note the effect;
Elsewhere I hear the cry of a regiment charging,
   (the young colonel leads himself
   this time with brandish'd sword,)
I see the gaps cut by the enemy's volleys,
   (quickly fill'd up, no delay,)
I breathe the suffocating smoke, then the flat clouds
   hover low concealing all;
Now a strange lull for a few seconds,
   not a shot fired on either side,
Then resumed the chaos louder than ever,
   with eager calls and orders of officers,
While from some distant part of the field
   the wind wafts to my ears
   a shout of applause, (some special success,)
And ever the sound of the cannon far or near,
   (rousing even in dreams a devilish exultation
   and all the old mad joy in the depths of my soul,)
And ever the hastening of infantry
   shifting positions, batteries, cavalry,
   moving hither and thither,
(The falling, dying, I heed not,
   the wounded dripping and red I heed not,
   some to the rear are hobbling,)
Grime, heat, rush,
   aides-de-camp galloping by or on a full run,
With the patter of small arms,
   the warning s-s-t of the rifles,
   (these in my vision I hear or see,)
And bombs bursting in air, and at night
   the vari-color'd rockets.
                                   —WALT WHITMAN

THE FACE

OF BATTLE

The advance of Sheridan's troops after the battle of
Winchester in September 1864. By A. R. Waud.

THE SIGNAL CORPS

This splendid picture by WILLIAM WAUD of signallin
across the James River at night in the autumn of 1864
was reproduced as a wood engraving in *Harper's Weekl*
on November 12, 1864. The printed result is so differen
—and so bad—that, as the Library of Congress says,
must be seen to be believed.

The officer at the telescope is reading messages fro
the high signal tower on the other side of the river whil
the man with the torches sends back the replies. Th
foot torch indicates the central position from which th
hand or flying torch moves to the right or left as it spell
out the words of the message. In the daytime, flags (on
of which can be seen below the foot torch) were used i
the same way. At night, the torch signals could be rea
ten or fifteen miles away.

The signal service began on July 2, 1860, with on
man, Major Albert J. Myer, who had invented a ne
method for signalling. He was sent to Indian country bu
was brought to Washington in July 1861 to train ne
personnel. Two of the officers who had worked with hi
joined the Confederacy. One was E. P. Alexander; th
other was J. E. B. Stuart.

The Signal Corps had its own field telegraph syste
but was impeded in its work by Stanton's insistence c
keeping control of all regularly established telegrap
lines.

This Signal Corps officer is stationed in the attic of
farmhouse near Williamsport, Maryland, to report deta
of the retreat of Lee's army from Gettysburg. The spurre
boots of the flagman on the roof can be seen. By EDW
FORBES.

Awaiting the enemy's fire

THE ARTILLERY

This gun crew, grimly waiting alongside their loaded cannon, are experts at their job. Each man has his own work to do: fire, swab out, load, aim, and fire again, all in rapid succession. It was the cannon that provided the thunderous accompaniment to Civil War battles. And at close range, using deadly grape or canister, the guns could cut holes through the ranks of advancing troops. Yet artillery was no longer the threat as it had been in Napoleon's day, for the greater range of the infantry's new rifles enabled good marksmen to pick off the gun crew, one by one. Nevertheless, the loud-roaring cannon were still greatly feared weapons, more useful perhaps for their awe-inspiring noise than for their long-range effectiveness. Unsigned.

Winslow Homer liked to draw cavalry; A. R. Waud drew all the services wit
equal skill; but EDWIN FORBES was in love with artillery, and his best drawing
are of the guns going into action. A six-horse team driven by three men draw
the limber and trailing fieldpiece. Two men sit on the ammunition chest (i
horse artillery they would be in the saddle so the gun could travel faster). A
soon as the firing position is reached, the gun is unlimbered and swung aroun
to face the enemy, while the horses take the ammunition chests to the rea
where they won't kill the men working the fieldpiece if they are exploded by
direct hit. And then the gunners go to work, firing three or four shots a minut

PLATE 97]   THE FACE OF BATTLE   81

It was a thrilling moment when the guns began to speak. General Joshua Chamberlain of the Twentieth Maine describes artillery in action: "It was splendid and terrible: the swift-served, bellowing, leaping big guns; the thrashing of the solid shot into the woods; the flying splinters and branches and tree-tops coming down upon the astonished heads; shouts changing into shrieks at the savage work of these unaccustomed missiles; then answering back the burst of fire oblique upon the left front of the battery, where there was a desperate attempt to carry it by flank attack; repulsed by sniper drawing to the left, and thus also leaving clear range for closer cutting projectiles, when now case shot and shell, now a blast of canister, poured into the swarming, swirling foe." By EDWIN FORBES.

The original wartime sketch by EDWIN FORBES. Made on
May 12, 1864, at Spotsylvania Court House in the rain as
more and more mud clings to the cannon wheels.

The worked-up, more carefully detailed drawing made after
the war from the picture shown above for one of the plates
in Forbes' series etchings of the Civil War.

And here, EDWIN FORBES, who knew the enduring value of a good action sketch, borrows his own material to use as the basis for an etching of an entirely different subject. The time is still the Wilderness Campaign, but the rain has stopped falling; it is night, and the pine woods have been set ablaze by shell fire. Troops on foot and horse march up a wide road to follow the wagons. But the cannon lumbering through the mud is still the one Forbes saw and sketched at Spotsylvania. (Note the uplifted whip and the bent angle of the limber and gun carriage.) The going must be easier now, for two men are now riding on the ammunition chest which was unoccupied in the two previous drawings.

THE PROGRESS OF ARTILLERY

The primitive state of Confederate artillery at the beginning of the war is seen in the first drawing where three large cannon provided with dolphins (handles for lifting) like those used in the eighteenth century are being dragged along the road by slow-moving cattle. The unsigned picture was made on July 8, 1861, less than two weeks before the first battle of Bull Run. It shows how desperately short of artillery the Confederates were at this time. They not only had very few guns, but were short of foundries, metal, machinery, and the skill to make them.

previous to the Battle of Bull's Run

Even as late as Cold Harbor in May and June 1864, field-pieces protected only by fence rows and rifle pits were still being used in open fighting as the second picture by A. R. WAUD shows.

But shortly afterward, when Grant and Lee settled down to a stalemate in the elaborate earthworks around Richmond and Petersburg, artillery as well as personnel was protected by carefully built fortifications. (Below) A. R. WAUD sketches a New York battery in the trenches before Petersburg some time in June or July 1864. A digging party is still at work, and picks and shovels are lying on the ground.

Art.y. Capt Ashby. 20 pounder parrott   A. R. Waud

Trottts field
July 2-1863   5⁻ᵃ
Capt Phillet
bringing off a gun
by prolonge

Sickles
Tree

TROSTLE's House
during the fight

Between the lines left centre
67
Sickles fell here   half the time

Caisson and battery horses — near
the grove of trees 2nd corps front the
scene of Pickett's charge — Gettysburg July 4th 1863 —
E Forbes

On July 2, 1863, the second day of Gettysburg, the fighting around the Trostle house reached dreadful intensity. The Ninth Massachusetts Battery was stationed near it. When a large body of Confederate skirmishers approached, there was no time to limber up the guns. Instead they were drawn back by pulling them by hand with the prolonge ropes. The Confederate advance was halted for a moment by canister; then the skirmishers came on until they were within six feet of the quickly reloaded guns. The blasts at close range blew some of the Confederates to pieces, but the others pressed on, bayonetting the cannoneers and shooting the men at the ammunition chests. Of the battery's 88 horses, 82 were killed. The two pictures at the left were made by CHARLES W. REED, a member of the battery. The upper one shows the use of the prolonge. The shell hole through the brick gable of the Trostle barn can still be seen today. Beyond the barn is the place where General Daniel Sickles lost his leg that day when hit by a cannon ball. The lower one shows the Trostle house, which still stands on the battlefield.

(Above) the wreckage of war after the great bombardment that preceded Pickett's charge. Sketched by EDWIN FORBES at Gettysburg on July 4, 1863.

MORTARS

Short stubby cannon that could hurl a larg
explosive shell high into the air so it would fa
behind the enemy's fortifications are of ver
ancient origin. Except that the bigger ones wer
made of cast iron rather than bronze and wer
mounted on wrought-iron riveted beds, the
remained basically unchanged in the Civil Wai
A really large one, like the famous 13-inch Dic
tator used against Petersburg, could cast a 20C
pound shell more than 4000 yards. Smaller one
like the two pictured here were effective fo
about a mile.

These drawings by A. R. WAUD show (above
an 8-inch mortar at Cold Harbor on June ?
1864, being cleaned out after firing; and (left
aiming a mortar.

Description on the back of sketch —

soldiers dummies ... in the works at Harrisons Landing

After their victory at First Manassas in July 1861, the Confederates fortified the field they had won. Not having enough cannon to fill the embrasures in the earthworks, they put logs of wood in place and painted them black so they looked like bristling guns. This simple trick worked so well that the Confederates used it at other places, Port Hudson among them, and here at Harrison's Landing on the James River, where well-constructed imitation field-pieces were put into position. To add a touch of realism, dummy soldiers were placed behind the "Quaker" guns. A. R. WAUD's description on the back of his sketch says that a photograph was taken of the scene before the figures were set up.

CAVALRY AND ARTILLERY

Taking guns by direct assault was one of the most dangerous assignments of the war. General Chamberlain describes what such an action involved: "There is no more picturesque and thrilling sight, no more telling, testing deed, than to 'take a battery' in front. Plowed through by booming shot; torn by ragged bursts of shell; riddled by blasts of whistling canister; straight ahead to the guns hidden in their own smoke; straight on to the red, scorching flame of the muzzles, the giant grains of cannon-powder beating, burning, sizzling into the cheek; then in upon them!—pistol to rifle-shot, saber to bayonet, musket-butt to hand-spike and rammer; the brief frenzy of passion; the wild 'hurrah!' then the sudden, unearthly silence; the ghastly scene; the shadow of death; the aureole of glory."

Here Custer's men capture three Confederate fieldpieces near Culpepper Court House on September 14, 1863. The dashing young general had his horse shot from under him in the cavalry charge. By EDWIN FORBES.

THE CAVALRY

Even to the men who were in it, cavalry was the most romantic of all the services. Their horses gave them companionship, devotion, and the ability to move farther and faster than anyone else in the army. Our modern conceptions of cavalry fighting, based on what we have seen in movies or TV, are largely erroneous. The horses did not immediately dash forward for a long charge; they would have been winded by the time they reached the enemy if they did. This contemporary description shows how a charge across an open field built up gradual momentum: "At the sound of the bugle we took the trot, the gallop, and then the charge. . . . We were welcomed by a fearful musketry fire, which . . . caused the entire brigade to oblique to the right. Instantly, officers cried: 'Forward! Forward!' The men raised their sabers, and responded to the command with deafening cheers. . . . We struck a blind ditch, but crossed it without breaking our front. In a moment we were face to face with the enemy. They stood as if awed . . . and in an instant broke in complete rout, our men sabering them as they vainly sought safety in flight." By EDWIN FORBES.

Here is the cavalryman in his most picturesque pose—running forward at full speed with drawn saber ready to strike
down the enemy. Drawing by CHARLES W. REED.

PLATE 113]   THE FACE OF BATTLE   93

An actual sketch, made on the spot by one
of the Special Artists of Frank Leslie's Illustrated Newspaper.

Mr. Leslie holds the copyright and reserves the exclusive right of publication.

The struggle for the guidon

And here is the cavalryman in close action. This superb drawing shows an attempt to capture the swallow-tailed guidon of the enemy by lunging at his throat with the hardly seen sword in the right hand while striking out with the bare left fist. The man carrying the Confederate guidon is doomed. His hand has let go his saber which dangles from a cord around his wrist. EDWIN FORBES drew this picture directly on wood December 8, 1862 so engraving could begin at once.

These two splendid sketches by WINSLOW HOMER of a cavalryman in the saddle seem to be made of the same model.

Winslow Homer had an artist's eye for significant detail. This sketch (at right) of a cavalryman's worn and wrinkled boots characterizes the hard-riding soldier who wore them.

A scouting party. By EDWIN FORBES.

Listening post. By EDWIN FORBES.

The cavalry skirmish line. By EDWIN FORBES.

Cavalryman awaiting orders. By EDWIN FORBES.

UNDER FIRE

No one enjoyed the experience of being reviewed when the enemy's shells were falling. Yet men and officers had to stand stiffly at attention and take their chances of being hit. Drawing by A. R. WAUD.

A halt for reforming the line of battle. When the ranks had been broken by shell and musket fire, the troops were ordered to reform their line. Here they do so at Antietam, looking out over their own dead. By EDWIN FORBES.

One of the bloodiest encounters of the war took place when
Gibbon's 24th Corps was ordered to take Fort Gregg, the
last Confederate stronghold before Petersburg, on April 2,
1865. By A. R. Waud.

Fighting in the woods was always deadly because friend
could often not be told from foe. This is a hand-to-hand
encounter between infantrymen of the 14th Brooklyn and
300 Confederate cavalrymen at Antietam. By A. R. Waud.

Advancing to the c...

One of the great action pictures of the wa

nfederates capturing disabled guns at Gaines Mills. By A. R. Wᴀᴜᴅ.

Three men—or more—are creeping forward, camouflaged with branches tied on to them. The two soldiers in the foreground know they are there—and they also know that the others have spotted them. Everyone is frozen into immobility, waiting to see who shoots first. Then the quiet woods will ring with rifle fire for a few moments until enough men have been killed or put out of action to make the lonely little skirmish decisive. And a few bodies left on the rocks for the turkey buzzards to find will mark the spot where men fought briefly and died. By J. T. E. HILLEN.

An actual sketch, made on the spot by one of the Special Artists of Frank Leslie's Illustrated Newspaper.

Mr. Leslie holds the copyright and reserves the exclusive right of publication.

Although the experience was probably one of lifelong humiliation to Lieutenant H. J. Segal, C.S.A., who is shown here being trapped by Union troops like a raccoon in a tree near Falls Church, Virginia, his capture was of such minor importance that the compilers of the 128-volume *Official Records of the Union and Confederate Armies* did not even bother to list his name in the index. But ARTHUR LUMLEY was there to make this drawing of the occasion and so preserved the hapless lieutenant's predicament for all posterity to see.

The North lost one of its ablest commanders when General Lyon was killed early
in the war. A West Pointer and a professional soldier, he was assigned to the
St. Louis Arsenal on February 6, 1861. During the summer he took to the field
to fight the powerful Confederate forces in Missouri. On August 10, 1861, he
was killed at the battle of Wilson's Creek. The official report of his death says:
"General Lyon's horse was killed, and he received a wound in the leg and one
in the head. He walked slowly a few paces to the rear and said, 'I fear the day
is lost.' But upon being encouraged that our troops could again be rallied, that
the disorder was only temporary, he passed over to the right of the center, where
our line seemed to be giving way, obtained another horse, and swinging his hat
in the air, led forward the troops, who promptly rallied around him. A few
moments later he was carried from the field dead." By HENRY LOVIE.

The battle of Munfordville, Kentucky, September 14, 1862, is almost forgotten, largely because it was overshadowed at that time by greater events developing in Maryland near Antietam Creek. Yet, as has been said, men are killed just as dead in a minor battle as in a major one.

The soldiers are Confederates from the 10th Mississippi Regiment under the command of Colonel R. A. Smith. The official report of this attempt to take the Federal fortifications along the river says that Smith "being entirely ignorant of the ground to be passed over, came within range of the enemy's guns from the right of their works and in front of the abatis of fallen trees, in a position where it was equally dangerous to advance or retreat, and immediately advanced against the works." Smith was badly wounded, and that day's attack failed, but General Braxton Bragg sent in a heavy supporting force, and the Union commander surrendered 4000 men on September 17. Unsigned.

The dramatic picture on the following two pages shows the vast tangle of men, horses, wagons, and artillery that characterized the battle of Shiloh or Pittsburg Landing on April 6, 1862. In this early major encounter the troops on both sides were green, and the casualties were unusually heavy. The circled copy gives details of distant Confederate batteries. Drawing by HENRY LOVIE.

The battle of Shiloh. By HENRY LO

Rebel Batteries Rebel Batteries 24 lbr Siege 2,10 lb Rifles

24 lbs Siege 64 lb heavy rifle

[ee previous page for caption.]

Sharpshooters, 18th Corps

When Grant began his long siege of Petersburg in 1864, the war was carried on
behind lines of earthworks that were very close together in many places. Fighting
settled down to mortar fire, occasional sorties, and continual sniping by well-
protected sharpshooters like these who could pick off a man with almost infallible
marksmanship. By A. R. WAUD.

Many photographs taken in modern times show in graphic detail what happens
when a man is hit by a bullet. But during the Civil War, cameras could not stop
action, so no such pictures were taken. Here CHARLES W. REED shows what
happens at the moment a bullet strikes. The occasion is along a creek known as
Hatcher's Run, located a few miles southwest of Petersburg. The time: any day
between February 5 and 10, 1865.

After nearly a year of intensive siege, Petersburg surrendered to Grant's Union forces at 4:28 A.M., Monday, April 3, 1865. Richmond surrendered a few hours later. Appomattox was less than a week away, and the war in Virginia was nearly over. For weeks Union troops marched through or were stationed in Petersburg. The little city had suffered from heavy shell fire, and there were gaping holes in many of the buildings and piles of bricks and rubble in the streets. Here Duryea's New York Zouaves are shown as they march down Sycamore Street. By CHARLES W. REED.

What was left of the Army of Northern Virginia made a desperate attempt to escape from Richmond and Petersburg but was stopped cold at Appomattox Court House by Grant's vastly larger force. There was some fighting early on the morning of April 9, 1865, but flags of truce were soon sent out. Here Captain R. M. Sims carries one of the white flags to young General George Armstrong Custer. Cloth was then so scarce in the Confederate army that Sims had to use a white towel with a red border. The same towel was used again when another officer rode out to stop firing in another part of the field. By A. R. Waud.

Cutting up the tree under which Grant & Lee met, for trophies —　　　A.R.W

A. R. Waud was apparently the only field artist who covered the final phases of the Appomattox Campaign. Here he draws a scene that shows how well the soldiers appreciated the historical significance of what was happening that day at Appomattox Court House. Officers quickly bought the furniture in the surrender room at the McLean house. The men had to be satisfied with souvenirs from the apple tree under which Lee had rested while waiting for Grant. After cutting off a few branches, "one of them, a lusty Maine fellow, seized an ax and within ten minutes every bit of the wood was cut up into convenient pieces for mementos. Not satisfied with this they dug up the roots and tendrils, and within an hour all that was left to mark the spot was a hole in the ground deep enough to bury a horse."

One of the most moving scenes in American history was the surrender of the weapons and battle flags of the Army of Northern Virginia at Appomattox on April 12, 1865. General Joshua Chamberlain, who was in charge of the operation, wrote: "We formed along the principal street, from the bluff bank of the stream to near the Court House on the left, to face the last line of battle, and receive the last remnant of the arms and colors of that great army which ours had been created to confront.... And now they move.... On they come, with the old swinging route step and swaying battleflags.... As each successive division masks our own, it halts, the men face inward towards us across the road, twelve feet away; then carefully dress their line.... They fix bayonets, stack arms; then remove cartridge-boxes and lay them down. Lastly—reluctantly, with agony of expression—they tenderly fold their flags, battle-worn and torn, blood-stained, heart-holding colors, and lay them down." By J. R. CHAPIN.

Regimental flags and the national colors were held so dear
by the soldiers that hundreds—and probably thousands—of
them died while proudly defending a bit of colored cloth that
meant more than life itself. By NATHAN B. WEBB.

The line of battle. Place and date unknown. By FRED E. RANSOM.

Confederate dead and wounded "after July 28," 1864, somewhere in Georgia. By G. T. E. HILLEN.

AFTERMATH

How solemn as one by one,
As the ranks returning worn and sweaty,
As the men file by where I stand,
As the faces the masks appear,
*   As I glance at the faces*
*   studying the masks . . .*
I see behind each mask that wonder
*   —a kindred soul.*
                        —WALT WHITMAN

A drawing by WINSLOW HOMER.

AFTERMATH

THE WOUNDED

Dreadful as war is, it is at least partly compensated for by the compassion it sometimes arouses in the hearts of men. Typical of the lulls between periods of active fighting is this scene of a soldier giving water to a wounded—and perhaps dying—victim of the lethal pieces of metal that have temporarily stopped flying over the field. By WINSLOW HOMER.

[PLATE 142] AFTERMATH 119

On the second day of the battle of the Wilderness (May 6, 1864), the dry woods caught fire, and the normal hell of battle literally became a raging inferno. Well men could get out of the way of the advancing flames, but the wounded who could not walk had to drag themselves along, be carried out, or perish in the smoke-filled woods. The screams of immobilized men, who were helpless when the fire reached them, drove others to incredible acts of heroism in rescue work. One of the best ways to get a man out was to put him in a blanket (wetted down if possible) suspended from four crossed rifles. The fires kept burning all night, lighting up the woods with a murky reddish glow. Men who lived through this experience at Wilderness felt that hell could hold no horrors for them. By A. R. WAUD.

Wounded escaping from the burning woods of the Wilderness —

THE WALKING WOUNDED

If he was not blinded, suffering from a bad head wound, or bleeding internally the soldier who did not have a smashed leg or hip was lucky, for he could a least walk or hobble away from the front to seek medical aid. Since there wei stragglers and deserters who also wanted to leave the area where the shooting wa going on, cavalry patrols barred the way. The horsemen bluntly put the query "Show blood," and if the man proved to be a malingerer he was arrested. Bu most of the soldiers streaming back from the front line were wounded, and mo of their wounds came from bullets, for bullets and not shells, bayonets, or saber were the most effective weapons of the Civil War. By WINSLOW HOMER.

AND THE WOUNDED WHO COULD NOT WALK

In this remarkable drawing made on June 3, 1862, after the battle of Fair Oaks, almost every method of conveying the seriously wounded to the rear is shown. Most prominent is the two-wheeled Finley ambulance which unfortunately was the one most commonly used in the early days of the war. It was structurally unsound and soon went to pieces; worse still, it shook its wounded passengers so badly that they cursed every jolt in the road. At the left is a horse carrying wounded men in two side panniers. In the foreground is a stretcher with a hood to protect the patient's face. Several ordinary stretchers are seen. And in the background is the train that will take the wounded to a permanent hospital. Any and all kinds of railroad cars have been pressed into service. Unsigned but probably by ARTHUR LUMLEY.

Citizen Volunteers assisting the wounded on the field of Battle   A. R. Waud —

Here, in all its horror, is a field dressing station at Antietam where the first attention is being given to the wounded as they come off the field. In the left foreground a surgeon has just completed an above-the-knee amputation on an improvised operating table. Chloroform or ether was usually but not always available for such work. At the right, citizen volunteers are loading a patient into an army wagon. In the background are more such wagons and the sorry freight they have just brought in. The yellow flag of the medical corps flies over the supply wagon at the extreme left. By A. R. WAUD.

This is another field dressing station, this time marked by the diamond-shaped indicator in the center of the picture. The place is at the White House on the way to Ely's Ford, and the time is May 2, 1863, during the battle of Chancellorsville. A rude cloth shelter has been erected for protection.

Actually, if infection and gangrene did not set in, men who had amputations stood a better chance of survival than those who were wounded internally. Unfortunately, however, the need for sanitation was not yet known. A soldier standing in front of the diamond marker is washing his hands—but not with any thought of making them surgically clean; the blood from many operations has made his fingers slippery. By EDWIN FORBES.

The unsigned painting (above) of Howard's Grove Hospital near Richmond, Virginia, was made by a Confederate soldier who had lost a leg in battle. *The Stranger's Guide . . . for the City of Richmond*, published in 1863, describes this hospital as being northeast of the city and says that it was intended primarily for the wounded from Mississippi regiments. The unsigned drawing (below) is a study made by a medical corps artist of a man dying from gangrene of the right arm.

The wounded got paid—but not for their wounds. Here a
patient recovering from a leg amputation in a tent hospital
is receiving his regular $13 a month from the paymaster.
An assistant holds a candle so the wounded man can see
while he signs a receipt. By PHILIP WHARTON.

PRISONERS OF WAR

These men being guarded by Union cavalry are prisoners, but, as can be see
by their uniforms and caps, they are Union soldiers. They are stragglers a
deserters who have been rounded up on February 10, 1863, during the reorgan
zation of the Union Army after its defeat at Fredericksburg. Its new commande
General Joseph Hooker, had been appointed on January 25. He was to last on
a few months. After his failure at Chancellorsville early in May, he was replac
by Meade only a few days before Gettysburg. By EDWIN FORBES.

and battle flags.
Rebel prisoners ... captured at
Chancellorsville, ... being taken to the rear by cavalry
and infantry guards.   Forbes May 3 '63

nd here, looking very much like the prisoners on the opposite page, is a batch
captives being marched to the rear on May 3, 1863, during the battle of
hancellorsville. But these are Confederates—or civilians suspected of being
onfederate sympathizers. What the future holds for these prisoners can be
en on the next eight pages. But difficult as life will be for the soldiers, it will
obably be even worse for the civilians, many of whom may be held for years
thout definite charges being brought against them. By EDWIN FORBES.

Two of the most famous Southern prisons were in Richmond. The tent camp on Belle Isle (below), which was for privates, and Libby Prison (on opposite page), which was for officers, were both dreaded by Union soldiers when they were captured. The Belle Isle camp was located on a small island in the James River. Only about four acres of low-lying ground were used—some of which was under water when the river flooded. Around the tent city was a low board railing where guards were stationed fifteen paces apart. The cannon on the hill were there to discourage any thought of a general uprising. Unsigned drawing made by a Union prisoner.

PLATE 153] AFTERMATH 129

Except for Andersonville, Libby was probably the best known of all Southern prisons. It was a solidly built tobacco warehouse converted into a jail for Union officers. There were huge rooms on several stories in which the prisoners sat idly day after day. The still existing records of admission show that nearly 125,000 men were confined at one time or another within its walls. The drawing by A. R. WAUD shows the prison after Richmond had fallen into Union hands. Confederate prisoners are waiting to be sent into the famous old "hotel."

Since Libby Prison was built for storing tobacco it was badly lighted and poorly ventilated. And it was usually much more crowded than the symbolic painting by DAVID G. BLYTHE on the following two pages indicates. No furniture or bedding was provided. The object standing on wooden horses in the center background is a coffin.

The Interior of Libby Prison. By DAVID G. BLYTHE

(See page 129 for caption.)

These four pictures by ALLEN C. REDWOOD show how men lived in a Union prison. (Above) Throwing bread to the prisoners. (Below) The man at the right is having a neck wound dressed.

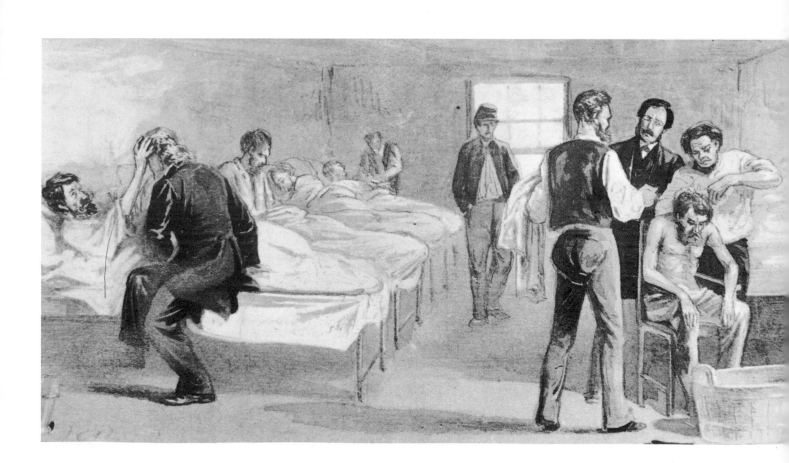

Very little is known about Redwood, but judging from his pictures he may have been a religious man, for he places great emphasis on the religious life of the prisoners.

Similarity of style, subject matter, and the crenelated wall
indicate that an artist named CRANE made both of these
pictures, even though the lower one is unsigned. (Above)
Sixteen mutineers of the New York Volunteer Engineers in
the Provost Guard Prison at Hilton Head, South Carolina.
(Below) The ringleader of the mutineers is forced to carry a
heavy weight on a wheelbarrow as punishment.

Flag of Truce

The most popular flag with both armies was the white flag of truce prominently displayed on one of the boats used for exchanging prisoners. Here Confederates are being transferred from a Federal flag-of-truce boat to a launch that will take them from open water near Norfolk to a landing place within their own lines. Since this is the summer of 1861, before the exchange of captives of war became formalized by the cartel of July 22, 1862, few prisoners could look forward to being exchanged at this time. Most exchange activity took place after the cartel and before Grant stopped the practice in 1864 when he said: "Every man we hold, when released on parole or otherwise, becomes an active soldier against us. . . . If we commence a system of exchange which liberates all prisoners taken, we will have to fight on until the whole South is exterminated." By A. R. WAUD.

The Bucktail's last Shot

Bethesda Church Va.

PRISONERS OF DEATH

This "Bucktail," hit by a bullet directly in the forehead, was killed instantly.
He was better off than the tens of thousands who died slowly and painfully from
the wounds of battle or from the effects of that greatest of all killers in the Civil
War—disease.

The Bucktails were men of the 13th Pennsylvania Regiment who got the name
from their habit of decorating their hats with a bit of deer's fur. Deer were
plentiful in the region they came from—the mountain wilderness in the northern
part of their state, and the regiment was recruited from men expert in the use
of a rifle. Drawing by EDWIN FORBES, made on June 8, 1864, after the battle of
Cold Harbor.

These six sorry-looking corpses, thrown one on top of the other to get them out
of the way, once were Confederate pickets posted along the ridge west of
Fredericksburg. They were killed in the terrible artillery bombardment from the
other side of the river when the Union batteries there were protecting the troops
who had to put pontoon bridges across the Rappahannock. These men were early
casualties in a battle that was to take the lives of thousands—mostly of Union
soldiers who fell in windrows when they tried to storm the practically impreg-
nable heights. Unsigned but probably by EDWIN FORBES.

Rebel Pickets dead, in Fredericksburg.
Pontoon Bridge, Union Batteries firing on the rebel works
back of the city= chosen the hill in the backround of Picture

An actual sketch, made on the spot by one
of the Special Artists of Frank Leslie's Illustrated Newspaper.

Mr. Leslie holds the copyright and reserves the exclusive right of publication.

BRAVE CAPTAINS AND

Flaunt out O sea your separate flags of nations!
Flaunt out visible as ever the various ship-signals!
But do you reserve especially for yourself
   and for the soul of man one flag above all the rest,
A spiritual woven signal for all nations,
   emblem of man elate above death,
Token of all brave captains
   and all intrepid sailors and mates,
And all that went down doing their duty,
Reminiscent of them,
   twined from all intrepid captains young or old,
A pennant universal, subtly waving all time,
   o'er all brave sailors,
All seas, all ships.

                     —WALT WHITMAN

NTREPID SAILORS

ᵰ June 27, 1861, while a landing party was attempt-
ᵧ to drive back a large Confederate force at Mathias
ᵢₙt, Virginia (only about 50 miles downstream
ᵐ Washington), Commander J. H. Ward of the
ᵗomac Fleet's *Freeborn* was killed by a musket ball
ᵉ fired his 32-pound bow gun. He was one of the
ₛt Naval casualties. By ARTHUR LUMLEY.

Ben Butler's amphibious operation at Cape Hatteras, August 1861. Troops are being landed in iron surf boats. By A. R. WAUD.

A blockade runner stranded on the beach in 1864. By D. J. KENNEDY.

The Navy doing aerial reconaissance work along the James River. Oddly enough, there was more aerial activity in the early part of the war than later on. During McClellan's campaign to take Richmond in 1862 by driving up the Peninsula from Yorktown, several balloons were used for observation. In some cases the balloonist telegraphed his reports to the ground. Here a balloon is being towed along the river to search areas held by the Confederates. By Arthur Lumley.

This Japanese-looking sketch by WILLIAM WAUD shows the *Louisiana*, an unfinished ironclad used as a floating battery, being blown up by the Confederates to prevent it from falling into Federal hands when Farragut ran up the Mississippi River to capture New Orleans in April, 1862.

Caricatures of the new Union sailors' uniforms authorized to be worn after December 21, 1863. Drawing by an unknown seaman.

Drawings made by CONRAD WISE CHAPMAN of seamen at the wheel of the British steamer *Alpha* on April 18, 1864, during a voyage from Charleston to Rome with Bishop Patrick N. Lynch, the Confederate special commissioner to the States of the Church.

Capture of contraband cargo on Lake Pontchartrain near New Orleans. Drawing by FRANK H. SCHELL.

The Federal monitor *Weehawken* sank on December 6, 1863, while moored to a buoy within the Charleston bar. A heavy load of shells made her so low in the water that it washed over her nearly submerged decks and flooded the hold. Twenty-four men were drowned. Unsigned.

The Confederate steamer *Ellis* in action, probably at the battle for Fort Hatteras, August 1861. Unsigned.

Loading a river steamer by torchlight on a rainy night at Montgomery, Alabama. Men struggle—and lose their footing—on the muddy bank as they try to get down to the boat. Two ladies are shielded from the rain by umbrellas held by gallant escorts. Undated and unsigned.

Federal officers on the *Jackson* use their telescopes to spot a blockade runner trying to make a night run. Unsigned.

Pikemen— away!!
Repelling boarders.

Eighteenth-century ways of naval fighting were still taught
in the Civil War. In this drill the seamen are armed with
pikes to repel a theoretical attempt to board the ship.

Gun drill on April 9, 1863, on board the *Richmond* while
at Baton Rouge. The city had been captured from the
Confederates the year before.

PLATE 178]   BRAVE CAPTAINS AND INTREPID SAILORS   147

Broadsword Exercise

Here and on the facing page are three primitives of sailor life by ROBERT WALTER WEIR, JR., who served on the U. S. Sloop of War *Richmond*. The drawing shown above oddly resembles the very modern work of Jean Cocteau.

One of the most often depicted American naval battles is that between the
Monitor and the *Merrimac.* There is good reason for this, for the historic combat
made every government in the world suddenly realize that the day of the wooden
fighting ship was gone forever.

When the Norfolk Navy Yard was burned in April, 1861, the U.S.S. frigate
Merrimac was only partly destroyed. The Confederates raised her sunken hulk,
sheathed it with iron, renamed the armored vessel the *Virginia,* and sent her into
Hampton Roads on March 8, 1862, to attack the Union naval ships there. She
sank the U. S. sailing frigate *Cumberland* and destroyed the *Congress* by setting
her on fire. The next day John Ericsson's iron *Monitor,* skeptically called a
"cheese-box-on-a-raft," arrived from New York, and after close-quarters combat,
the *Merrimac* retired to Norfolk. This unsigned picture of the history-making
engagement bears a label saying that it was "painted on the spot."

Although the wooden U. S. sloop of war *Richmond* played a relatively minor part in the battle of Mobile Bay on August 5, 1864, ROBERT WALTER WEIR, JR. was aboard her and made this drawing from personal observation. The giant Confederate ironclad ram *Tennessee* was the most powerful ship guarding the bay when Farragut's fleet of fourteen wooden vessels and four iron monitors sailed in at dawn. The wooden *Hartford* and the *Richmond* ran past the iron-plated ram, firing as they went. For twenty minutes they poured their heaviest shot into her, but inflicted no great damage. One of the Federal monitors had been sunk by torpedoes, but the others, aided by the wooden ships, took on the *Tennessee*. One after another they rammed her and blasted away with their big guns until the Confederate ram surrendered. She was repaired and added to the Union fleet.

This general mixup of ships in the Mississippi River with Memphis in the background was an unconventional naval battle in which fast river steamers, hastily strengthened by extra heavy timbers, rammed and fired at eight Confederate ships and knocked out or captured all but one, the *Earl Van Dorn*, which escaped. Oddly enough, the idea of converting ordinary river boats into improvised wooden rams came not from the Navy but from the Army. It was conceived and carried out by Colonel Charles Ellet, Jr., an engineer by profession and a member of a well-known Army family. Thousands of people lined the river banks at Memphis to watch the great spectacle. When the Confederate fleet was defeated, the city surrendered. Painting by ALEXANDER SIMPLOT.

And this grand melee of ships and forts whanging away at each other is a pictorial representation by J. JOFFRAY of Farragut's fleet running past Forts St. Philip and Jackson. Sloops of war, fire rafts, river steamers, mortar boats, and armored rams all took part in this fierce engagement which was preceded by five days of heavy bombardment. The Federal fleet succeeded in passing the forts and on April 25 compelled New Orleans to surrender. Three days later the forts also capitulated. The unfinished ram *Louisiana*, which had withstood the fire of the Federal fleet, had remained tied up close to shore during the entire battle. Her officers now set her on fire. When the flames reached her powder magazine she blew up, as shown on Page 142.

South Carolina was the first state to secede, and its largest city, Charleston, was regarded by Northerners as the fountain head of secession. Consequently, intensive and unceasing efforts were made to capture or destroy the city that was protected by Fort Sumter and a ring of defensive works around the harbor. As the war progressed, the Federals brought in more and more big guns to reduce the citadel of rebellion. And the Confederates, always short of artillery of any kind, determinedly shipped to Charleston the best and biggest cannon they could obtain. Since they had almost no facilities for casting and machining heavy guns, the cannon sent to Charleston's defense consisted largely of weapons captured in United States arsenals at the beginning of the war or brought in through the blockade from England. Drawing by CONRAD WISE CHAPMAN, dated October 29, 1863.

PLATE 184] BRAVE CAPTAINS AND INTREPID SAILORS 153

At the right-hand entrance to Charleston Harbor were Fort Moultrie and Battery Marion where some of the very largest Confederate coastal guns were placed to prevent hostile ships from running in. This is one of the big guns in Battery Marion sketched by CONRAD WISE CHAPMAN on November 14, 1863, after Fort Sumter (seen at the right) had been battered for months by concentrated artillery fire from Federal ships and coastal batteries. At the far left smoke is rising from the Union batteries on Morris Island as they hurl giant projectiles at the city. Activity at this time, however, was relatively slight, for Federal engineers were busy mounting new guns and mortars. During the summer the famous "Swamp Angel," an 8-inch Parrott rifled cannon located less than five miles from Charleston, had sent incendiary shells loaded with Greek fire into the heart of the city. Because of overloading, the gun burst after firing 36 shots.

The forty-foot-high stone walls of Fort Sumter were from five to ten feet thick, so the big guns in the lower tiers were mounted in pie-shaped casements where they could be swung in narrow arcs to fire through small circular openings in the masonry. The Federal fleet and coastal artillery pounded the island fort with eleven- and fifteen-inch shells that gradually reduced the huge building to a shapeless pile of rubble. But the Union forces were never able to take the massive structure that guarded the entrance to Charleston Harbor. The city and its formidable defenses passed quietly from Confederate to Union hands on February 18, 1865, the day after Sherman's army captured and burned the state capital, Columbia. By CONRAD WISE CHAPMAN.

This unsigned sketch shows a Union water battery manned by gunners from the 7th Connecticut Regiment shelling a Confederate water battery at Yorktown on May 4, 1862, during the Peninsular Campaign. In this battle for possession of the historic town which had seen the surrender of Cornwallis' British army in 1781, troops in blue and gray dug new trenches across the old Revolutionary earthworks and fought on ground their ancestors had jointly defended against a foreign invader. A Confederate withdrawal up the Peninsula had been ordered on May 3, so the cannonading shown here was probably a precautionary measure before Federal troops entered the abandoned town. The smoke in the distance comes from an ammunition warehouse which the Confederates had set on fire.

Beat! beat! drums!
  —blow! bugles! blow!
Through the windows—through doors
  —burst like a ruthless force,
Into the solemn church,
  and scatter the congregation,
Into the school where the scholar is studying;
Leave not the bridegroom quiet
  —no happiness must he have
  now with his bride,
Nor the peaceful farmer any peace,
  ploughing his field
  or gathering his grain,
So fierce you whirr and pound you drums
  —so shrill you bugles blow.
                    —WALT WHITMAN

When the battle of Fredericksburg was fought in December 1862, Union troops occupied the lower streets of the heavily shelled town while fighting continued on the heights to the west. The soldiers, like all soldiers in all wars, made themselves at home with what they could salvage from the ruins. Drawing by ARTHUR LUMLEY.

INTO THE HOMES AND

PLATE 187] INTO THE HOMES AND HEARTS OF THE PEOPLE 157

HEARTS OF THE PEOPLE

After New Orleans was occupied by Federal forces in April 1862 and General Benjamin F. Butler was made its military governer, a considerable number of Louisiana citizens suspected of being active Confederate sympathizers were arrested and imprisoned. Unsigned.

On June 28, 1863, when Lee's army was advancing toward Gettysburg, the people of Baltimore were so frightened by the thought of invasion that they erected barricades in the streets. By EDWIN FORBES.

On August 21, 1863, Lawrence, Kansas, was raided by the Confederate guerrilla William C. Quantrill. With 450 horsemen he burned the town and killed nearly 200 men, women, and children. By SHERMAN ENDERTON.

As the war progressed, cotton became scarce and high priced. Here FRANK VIZETELLY shows cavalrymen stopping Confederates who are trying to burn cotton to prevent it from falling into Federal hands. The scene is on the border of Tennessee and Mississippi.

Early in the war and only a few miles from the place where the first Negro slaves were sold in America in 1619, the famous term "contraband of war" as a euphemistic phrase for escaped slaves seeking the protection of the Union Army, was coined by the ubiquitous Ben Butler. In May 1861, three runaways came to Fortress Monroe by boat. When a Confederate major, acting as agent for their owner, demanded their return, Butler told him that he was detaining the Negroes as "contraband of war" and was going to put them to work on the batteries. After that, fleeing slaves came swarming to the Union armies by the thousands, using every possible means of conveyance to reach their goal. Here EDWIN FORBES draws a group of fugitives entering the Union lines in an ancient farm wagon (called a "schooner") drawn by a horse, a mule, and an ox.

PLATE 193] INTO THE HOMES AND HEARTS OF THE PEOPLE 161

One of the few pictures the noted artist EASTMAN JOHNSON painted about the war is this one entitled "A Ride for Liberty." It shows a Negro slave, his wife, and two children running away from his master's home on a "borrowed" horse.

The problem of what to do with the fugitive slaves who came to the Union armies expecting to be declared free was one of the most vexatious of the war. Generals who were over-eager to give the slaves their freedom were sharply brought to account by Washington. Others refused to admit the slaves, and still others simply avoided taking a stand on the matter.

In the summer of 1862, Negroes were allowed to enlist in the Army, and several Negro regiments were soon formed. The young Boston socialite, Robert Gould Shaw, died on the beaches of Charleston while leading one of them.

Numerous pictures have been made of the deathbed of Lincoln. Actually, no artist was present to sketch the scene, but this drawing by HERMANN FABER, a technical draftsman at the Army Medical Museum, seems to be the first one made after the event. Faber entered the Petersen house across the street from Ford's Theatre as soon as the slain President's body was removed. At that time nothing in the narrow little hall bedroom had been disturbed so he could record the setting; later he filled in the people. The Army officer seated in a chair looking at his watch to determine the exact moment of death (7:22 A.M. April 15, 1865) is Surgeon General Joseph K. Barnes. The bearded man on the bed taking the dying man's pulse is Dr. Robert King Stone, the President's personal physician. Stanton stands on the right; Gideon Welles is seated at the far left, while Charles Sumner stands with clasped hands in back of Lincoln's head.

This sketch of the interior of Ford's Theatre made by A. R. WAUD soon after the assassination gives a clear picture of the setting for that world-famous event. As a guide to the engraver, he has put people in the picture. A figure representing Booth stands on the stage where he broke his leg when he leaped out of the upper right box. In the box itself Lincoln is at the far right with Mrs. Lincoln alongside him. The woman visible in the other box opening is Miss Clara Harris who is sitting on a sofa with her fiancé, Major Henry Rathbone.

The stage was never used for theatrical performances after that tragic night. The building stood empty for many months, then the government acquired it for the Record and Pension Bureau of the War Department. On June 9, 1893, the interior collapsed, killing 22 people and injuring 68 others. The restored structure is now the Lincoln Museum.

The funeral of Abraham Lincoln was the most impressive ever held in the United States. His body was taken by special train from Washington to Springfield, Illinois, his home town. When it arrived there on May 3, 1865, it was placed on this catafalque on the second floor of the State House in Representatives' Hall where Lincoln had made some of his most important speeches. Some 75,000 people, many of whom had known the dead President, filed through the building to pay their last respects.

Plate 197]   INTO THE HOMES AND HEARTS OF THE PEOPLE   165

The more important prisoners arrested for their suspected part in the plot to kill Lincoln were at first confined in monitors anchored in the Potomac. When one of them tried to beat out his brains against the iron walls of the monitor, canvas hoods were put on their heads. This picture of them being transferred to the Old Arsenal Penitentiary was made by its commandant, Colonel JAMES G. BENTON.

Funeral procession, 1865. Unsigned but probably by A. R. WAUD.

ASHES OF SOLDIERS

Ashes of soldiers South or North,
As I muse retrospective murmuring a chant in thought,
The war resumes, again to my sense your shapes,
And again the advance of the armies.
Noiseless as mists and vapors,
From their graves in the trenches ascending,
From cemeteries all through Virginia and Tennessee,
From every point of the compass
    out of the countless graves,
In wafted clouds, in myriads large,
    or squads of twos or threes or single ones they come,
And silently gather round me.

Now sound no note O trumpeters,
Not at the head of my cavalry
    parading on spirited horses,
With sabres drawn and glistening,
    and carbines by their thighs,
    (ah my brave horsemen!
My handsome tan-faced horsemen!
    what life, what joy and pride,
With all the perils were yours.)

Nor you drummers, neither at reveillé at dawn,
Nor the long roll alarming the camp,
    nor even the muffled beat for a burial,
Nothing from you this time
    O drummers bearing my warlike drums.

But aside from these and the marts of wealth
    and the crowded promenade,
Admitting around me comrades
    close unseen by the rest and voiceless,
The slain elate and alive again,
    the dust and debris alive,
I chant this chant of my silent soul
    in the name of all dead soldiers.

Faces so pale with woundrous eyes,
    very dear, gather closer yet,
Draw close, but speak not.

Phantoms of countless lost,
Invisible to the rest henceforth become my companions,
Follow me ever—desert me not while I live.
                                        —WALT WHITMAN

INDEX